THE TOTAL
MacGyver
MANUAL

THE TOTAL

MacGyver
MANUAL

FOREWORD BY
PETER LENKOV

INTRODUCTION BY
LUCAS TILL

SCIENCE BY
DR. RHETT ALLAIN

TEXT BY
IAN CANNON

weldon**owen**

CONTENTS

**CHAPTER 3:
TRAPS + GETAWAYS**

CHAPTER 4:
DISTRACTIONS + DEFENSES

CHAPTER 5
REPAIRS + RESCUES

FOREWORD

Luckily, you do not need a Swiss Army knife to open this foreword, but if you did, I am guessing that since you are holding this book in your hands, you might just happen to have one on you. Well done for thinking of every scenario.

Growing up in Montreal, you get used to the kind of bad weather that keeps you inside and glued to the television. And from my family's sofa, I was able to travel the world and escape to foreign lands that were warm and welcoming, far from those cold, harsh Canadian winters. And like any lifelong passion that you nurture with devotion and time, I immersed myself in front of that glowing box, watching everything from *Magnum, P.I.* to *M*A*S*H**, and of course—one of my personal favorites—*MacGyver*.

Every Monday night I'd tune in to see what new, crazy scheme Mac would cook up to escape a seemingly inescapable situation. He was what I called "a thinking man's hero." Mac could stop the bad guys in their tracks, recover the assets, and save the world, all without having to use a gun. MacGyver used his ingenuity to solve problems, proving that no matter how difficult or complex they were, there was always a way to think his way through them. And so important for a young Canadian television nerd like myself, he made being a geek cool. Like MacGyver, I loved working with my hands and tinkering with machinery (mostly bikes though—nothing as serious as, say, a rocket thruster). In a crowded

landscape of TV cops and PI's, I was thrilled to finally find a hero I could identify with.

When my friends at CBS came to me in 2016 to ask if I would write and produce a new take on *MacGyver*, I was filled with all the emotions Mac must have felt on each mission: excitement, trepidation, and a sense of adventure. I was honored to work on the new series with one of the original producers, the legendary Henry Winkler, one of my childhood heroes. (Really, who didn't want to be the Fonz growing up?!) My priorities were to make sure that we stayed true to the mythology, and maintain the cultural zeitgeist they tapped into with the original series.

As a writer, I knew I had enough experience to take a stab at this—but in all honesty, I knew nothing about the science that makes *MacGyver* so unique. (And since we're being honest, I can tell you I was a horrible student. Math and science were not my friends.) When it came to the physics and science of the show, I was just like any *MacGyver* fan, simply in awe of what a piece of chewing gum, some duct tape, and a paper clip can do with a little imagination and a whole lot of resourcefulness. All this is to say, I could dream up a scenario and a way out of it, but I needed

help rooting those ideas in reality. Enter South Eastern Louisiana University Physics professor and *MacGyver* superfan, Rhett Allain; this literal genius became our technical consultant. Rhett's mastery of physics, engineering, and logic were paramount to making each and every episode believable and authentic. I wanted to ensure that every time a viewer saw Mac do his thing, it was 100% possible. With these crucial Mac Hacks and MacGyverisms, Angus MacGyver becomes the smartest man on the planet.

The last piece of the puzzle in bringing MacGyver to life was finding the perfect actor to play him. It quickly became clear that Lucas Till is everything we could want in a leading man. He has the ability to convey complicated scientific principles in just a few words and motions, a relatable everyman quality, and a spectacular sense of humor. And while he probably couldn't dismantle a dirty bomb outside of the show (at least without Rhett's help), Lucas has mastered the original charm and wit of Angus MacGyver that makes this character so endearing.

But perhaps the most important reason this franchise is a success is you—the fans. We are so grateful that you have embraced our family at the Phoenix Foundation, and tuned in every Friday night. We make this show, working tirelessly to perfect everything in it—including all of Mac's tricks—for you.

Improvise or Die,

PETER M. LENKOV
Executive Producer, *MacGyver*

P.S. I am sure it says something like "Please do not try this at home" somewhere in here, but honestly, if you are ever held hostage by terrorists in a far-off land, it couldn't hurt to try.

INTRODUCTION

It seems like my tenure as TV's globe-trotting scientist was preordained. My father, John Till, is a Black Hawk pilot and Lieutenant Colonel in the United States Army, who also happened to have had the nickname "MacGyver."

My dad was not only the handiest guy to have around (Make a DIY smoker—check! Identifying wood-burning foliage on a hunting trip—check! Catching a pesky badger—check, check!), he was skilled in all forms of survival, constructing assorted contraptions, and an all-around good dad. My mom, Dana Brady Till, is a technical director and an accomplished chemist for an environmental laboratory, and my go-to resource for pronunciations of all things chemical. With this pedigree, it was only logical that one day their actor son would play an iconic TV know-it-all.

In 2016, CBS decided to make a rebooted version of the classic series. They were looking for a new MacGyver and I happened to be looking for a job, so one thing led to another and after a meeting and an audition, I got the call that I had been cast. I felt like Mac at the start of every mission: I know I can do this, but I need the best team with me in order to succeed.

I mean, how do you prepare to know, well, everything?! Do I binge on YouTube videos? Read a library of how-to manuals? Lucky for me, our showrunner Peter Lenkov was there to walk me through the *MacGyver* mythology, revering every aspect of the character from the leather jacket to the ever-present Swiss Army knife. (There were many conversations about my hairstyle as well, but that has nothing to do with science and everything to do with television optics).

We started filming in Atlanta, my hometown, and when you work on a television series, you, and everyone around you, move at lightning speed in order to make the airdate. When I get a script, I memorize the scientific jargon, then rehearse the dialogue scenes with a partner. When I get to set, I work through each Mac Hack and integrate it into what I've already learned. There are about six Mac Hacks per episode. Thanks to our prop team, Katie Guanci and Sean Macomber, I learn how to manipulate all the components so that I look like I know what I am doing. Sometimes I have to describe the science as I act; luckily, our technical consultant and staff genius, Rhett Allain, helps the writers craft a 100% possible way for us to save the world. Other times I can just do my MacGyver thing while other members of the Phoenix team joke about my geek brain = less dialogue for me to memorize!

Pretending to be a super-genius, even with the Herculean efforts of our team behind-the-scenes, is not always easy but is a lot of fun . . .

and sometimes can get pretty messy. In episode 110 ("Pliers"), I showed a group of students in a science class how to make elephant toothpaste (a combination of hydrogen peroxide, water, dish soap and yeast). It's a weird and fascinating chemical reaction where the whole thing just oozes over the sides and makes for a great visual (I later make an even bigger version to take down the bad guys). I love working with kids on set, and luckily, they had a lot of patience for me that day because after numerous takes, I still couldn't get the timing just right, but eventually, we got the shot. It's a Mac Hack you can actually try at home without purchasing uranium or potentially setting your house on fire!

I'm proud that we can pull off these scientific feats on a weekly basis, and we must be doing a realistic job: whenever I meet fans, they ask me physics and engineering questions that I would be more than happy to Google for them. No, I don't know if you can use cooking oil in your gas tank, and no, I can't pick a lock with a paper clip. But, if you'd like to see a few parlor tricks I've learned using toothpicks and forks, I'm your guy. The most important lesson I've learned: leave the real science to the real scientists.

All I know is, every week I get to carry a Swiss Army knife, chew a few pieces of gum, and save the world, all because of a bunch of very smart people you never see behind the scenes . . . and because of you, the fans. We are grateful to have you with us every time I defuse a bomb, save a town from disaster, and escape from the bad guys.

Just don't test me on the periodic table or how to slip out of a pair of handcuffs—I will be reading this book just like you.

Warmly,

LUCAS TILL
MacGyver, of CBS's *MacGyver*

THE PHOENIX FOUNDATION

In the words of Matilda Webber, Director of Field Operations, the Phoenix Foundation is "tasked with taking down enemies of the state, stopping acts of terrorism, and saving lives all around the world wherever they are imperiled." Formerly known as the Department of External Services (and other names before) it's staffed by highly trained scientists and technicians, and some of the finest members of the military and other government agencies. Far from just another government think tank or military branch, the Phoenix Foundation's emphasis on science combined with tactical training produces some of the most successful covert field teams in the world, tackling a variety of missions too unusual or politically sensitive for the larger agencies.

ANGUS MACGYVER

FIELD AGENT / EXPLOSIVES EXPERT
HEIGHT: 5'10"
LANGUAGES: English, Italian, Mandarin, Ukrainian

The biggest brain in the Phoenix Foundation, MacGyver graduated early from MIT before enlisting with the Army. Although highly averse to firearms, he served two years in Explosive Ordnance Disposal in Afghanistan, where his unusual approach made him a legend and saved countless lives. MacGyver's time in EOD also led to a friendship with Jack Dalton, a Delta Force operator who acted as Mac's overwatch sniper. Honorably Discharged with an excellent performance record, MacGyver was quickly recruited into the DXS—later to become the Phoenix Foundation. A genius intellect and believer in a creative solution to any problem, MacGyver applies that philosophy to ideas ranging from paperclips to plastic explosives.

JACK DALTON

FIELD AGENT / COMBAT EXPERT
HEIGHT: 5'11"
LANGUAGES: English, Dutch, French, Russian

The brawn to MacGyver's brain, Dalton is an expert combatant and tactician. He's also a former Texas rodeo whipcracking champion, Bruce Willis memorabilia collector, and pop-culture fan. A former CIA and Delta Force operative trained in stealth and subterfuge, he still prefers (okay, enjoys) a "kick the door down" approach. His demeanor usually runs from "confident" to "brash," but in the end, he always has MacGyver's back. If you can shoot, fly, or drive it, Jack Dalton is your go-to guy: A highly skilled wheelman who always carries a gun (and at least one backup).

RILEY DAVIS

DATA ANALYST / EXPERT HACKER
HEIGHT: 5'4"
LANGUAGES: English, Ukrainian

A frighteningly skilled hacker, Davis was recruited to the
Phoenix Foundation by Dalton, who first knew her through
a relationship with her mother. Formerly a "black hat"
hacker serving time in a supermax prison—a security level
reserved for the worst types of criminals, or individuals
who pose a grave threat to national or global security—
she's since used her abilities to aid the team in missions
worldwide. Strongly opinionated on personal liberty and
privacy, Davis has a very, very long government file . . .
one that is highly redacted and has a great deal more text
blacked out than legible.

WILT BOZEMAN

PROSTHETICS AND EFFECTS SPECIALIST
HEIGHT: 5'6"
LANGUAGES: English, Mandarin

MacGyver's friend since childhood, Wilt Bozer was hired to
the Phoenix Foundation after he discovered the true nature
of Mac's work as a secret agent. His skills as a filmmaker
and prop builder make him an ideal prosthetics and effects
specialist, though he's something of a jack-of-all-trades
himself by way of his shared childhood with Mac. Bozer
also shares responsibility for a few "incidents" in their youth,
including one involving a small nuclear reactor and a now-
long-gone high-school football field. (It's a long story.)

MATILDA WEBBER

OPERATIONS DIRECTOR
HEIGHT: 3'11"
LANGUAGES: English, [Classified]

Formerly of the CIA, Director Webber is a no-nonsense leader
with an intimidating, but results-driven, demeanor. (She even
reputedly hung up on Vladimir Putin once, before he called her
back ten minutes later to apologize.) She's determined to ensure
the Foundation runs smoothly, and completes its missions with
maximum effectiveness and efficiency. Sharing a history with
Dalton as his superior in the CIA before a failed operation forced
him to quit, she greatly prefers to operate by the book, but
tolerates and accepts MacGyver's unconventional methods.

YOUR ESSENTIAL TOOLKIT

The Phoenix Foundation doesn't necessarily issue expensive firearms or high explosives to all its top agents; in fact, it doesn't always have to. With the tutorials in this text, you'll soon learn how almost any household item can serve the cause of freedom. Item Zero, of course, is you—your intelligence, experience, resourcefulness, and all-around wits. Along with that, these here are your true tools for victory. Just make sure you always, always have item number one on this list.

SWISS ARMY KNIFE
The one tool to make and use all other tools, the Swiss Army Knife is one thing you'll likely need to get through your mission. Make sure you've got one with screwdrivers (flat and Phillips at least), a saw, and pliers or scissors to start with.

LIGHTER
There are a lot of flammable items in the world, and you never know what needs to be set alight in order to complete your work. A simple pack of matches is a good start, but a lighter can last a lot longer and won't be ruined if it gets wet.

CANDLE
From providing illumination to work in a dark space, to lighting up someone's birthday cake, you can do a lot with candles—and with the wax they're made from.

ALUMINUM FOIL
A favorite of household kitchens (and conspiracy theorists) everywhere, tinfoil's various properties mean that you can do a lot more with it than just wrap up leftovers or protect your brain from mind-control rays.

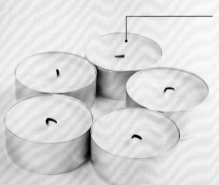

CHEWING GUM

It's portable, tacky, lightweight, and along with its various technical uses, some brands come individually wrapped in a little piece of foil—a two-for-one deal in the field. And, if nothing else, you can use it to freshen your breath.

BATTERIES

Plenty of improvised tools in the field will need a power source, and there's nothing that provides power in your hand the same way as a battery. 9-volt and AA type batteries are the most portable, though D-cells and larger will give you more energy.

DUCT TAPE

The main character in The Martian calls duct tape "magic," saying it's deserving of worship, and I'm inclined to agree. You don't have to bring a whole roll of this stuff with you in the field, but a good length of it wound around a small stick or some other spool will serve you well.

ROPE

For tying up bad guys, rigging endless numbers of devices and traps, rope is absolutely necessary, whether it's a coil of thumb-thick climbing rope or slender paracord.

PAPERCLIP

One of the most versatile items in the world, you may find more uses for this than you think. What can you do with a paperclip, you ask? What can't you do?

CHAPTER 1

BREAK-INS
+ BREAKOUTS

A FORCE OF NATURE

Most people would give up if they found their way blocked by a high fence topped with razor wire—or if they were locked in a tiny jail cell, or tied to a chair. But not Angus MacGyver. Armed with little more than the contents of his pockets, his flair for innovation, and the laws of physics, he'll find a way.

You might not have expected to see physics on a list of Mac's essential tools, but the fact is that if you really want to understand how he pulls off some of these stunts, you'll need to grasp the basic principles of physics. But not just physics. You will also need chemistry, biology, and math . . . and that's just for starters. But don't worry! These subjects are a lot more fun than you may remember from high school. Here are some of the most important concepts you'll see at work in the pages that follow.

FORCE + MOTION When you push on wall, that's an example of a force. Oh, did you know what else is considered a force according to physics? The gravitational force of the Earth pulling down on you. MacGyver kicking open a door (see item 008). Even sliding a book across a table involves force. These are all forces. But what do forces actually do?

The fundamental nature of a force on an object is to change that object's motion. Forces don't make things move, forces make things move differently. If you push on a ball with a constant force, it will constantly speed up. If you push sideways on a moving ball, it will constantly change direction. Yes, you can have a constant change.

But why don't we notice these changes in motion all the time? The answer is friction.

FRICTION If you want to climb the outside of a building using a vacuum cleaner (see item 014), you are going to need friction. It's not the

suction that prevents you from falling, it's the friction. Friction is a force between two interacting surfaces, and since just about everything has a surface, friction pops up everywhere. The strength of this frictional force gets greater when the two surfaces are pushed together and its direction is perpendicular to the surface. If you push someone against a wall with a long pole, you will increase the frictional force. In fact, the frictional force can get large enough for that human to run up a wall just like MacGyver did.

TORQUE We like to think of forces as pushes and pulls that change the motion of an object. But what if you want to rotate an object? This is where the idea of torque becomes useful—it's essentially the rotational version of force. You probably already understand torque on an operational level. When you go to open a door, you don't push at the hinge. No, you push on the other edge of the door, at the handle. This is because torque depends on both the pushing force and the distance from the pivot point. Pushing farther

away from the hinge increases the torque and makes it easier to open that door.

You also need torque when picking a lock—one of the most basic MacGyver hacks. By applying torque to the lock cylinder you can get the lock pins to become stuck. Sticking pins one by one is the key to a successful lock pick.

ENERGY Suppose you want to take an oxygen tank and launch it at a locked door, say—just for the sake of conversation—with an improvised ballista built from a metal bed frame and some springs (see item 013). But why on Earth would you want to do that? Well, if you are MacGyver, there is surely a reason.

Now for the real question: How far back would you pull the tank and what kind of springs would you need? This is the calculation that MacGyver needs to make to successfully launch this projectile. This is actually a classic physics problem that uses the idea of energy. You can think of energy as a different way to look at interacting objects. Mathematically it works, so we

just keep on using it.

For the case of the ballista, there are really two types of energy to be concerned with: kinetic and spring potential. The kinetic energy depends on the mass and final speed of the oxygen tank. When this tank goes flying across the room, its energy comes from the stretched springs which have spring potential energy. The stiffer the spring and the more it is compressed, the greater the stored energy. In the end, energy is conserved. The amount of spring potential energy must be equal to the increase in kinetic energy.

Of course there are other types of energy. One that you will see quite often is thermal energy. This is the energy associated with the change in temperature of things. Sometimes you might want to get something super hot, like so hot that you can melt metal. You can get this much thermal energy through a chemical reaction that happens with thermite (see item 012). But let me tell you right now—don't mess with this stuff. It's not just hot, but really really dangerous hot.

PAPERCLIP

You can find this simple office-essential item pretty much everywhere. (In fact, there's literally a punch bowl full of paperclips in the Field Director's office.) What can you do with this little piece of springy steel? A lot!

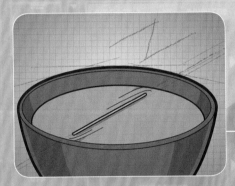

CREATE A COMPASS
Steel is ferromagnetic, and with a little work using a magnet and a bowl of water, you can improvise a compass— and, like any other compass, it'll do double duty pinpointing other strong electromagnetic fields nearby.

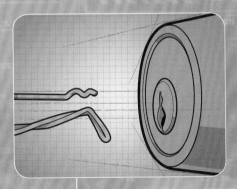

PICK A LOCK
From padlocks to handcuffs, Phoenix Foundation operatives run into a lot of locks— and a paperclip can be a handy lockpick.

GO FISH

No fish hook? It's not as sharp and lacks a barb, but unbend a paperclip, and you'll have a hook instantly, whether you're looking to snag a trout or a zipper tab.

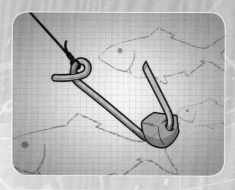

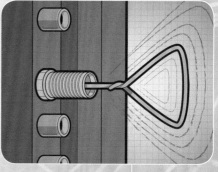

BOOST A SIGNAL

The coaxial port on the back of a TV or radio can hook up to an antenna, but if you're lacking one, bend a paperclip into an open simple shape (a triangle for example) and insert it into the pinhole in the port to boost reception!

SHORT A CIRCUIT

Since steel paperclips conduct electricity, and can be used as a makeshift fuse, you can also use one to disable electrical systems—if you know which two points to connect. (Better brush up on those Cold War–era missile schematics!)

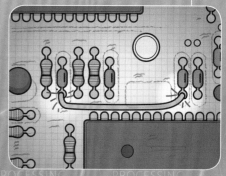

BRIDGE A BLOWN FUSE

Fuses are meant to blow out if the electric current in the circuit is too strong, so this isn't exactly safe, but if you need to keep an electrical connection, a paperclip can do the trick. Just be cautious; paperclips don't blow like fuses, so they'll present a fire or shock hazard.

HANDCUFF ESCAPE

As a Phoenix operative, personal resourcefulness is your most important tool—that said, a simple short length of metal goes a long way. Yes, we're talking paperclips: they're ubiquitous, innocuous, and frankly wondrous. Now, at some point, you or someone else may end up in cuffs. Luckily, while handcuffs are hindering, even if you can't get a key from your captor, you can still find your way to freedom using your little buddy. Handcuffs use a pair of metal pieces in their mechanism, called lock bars, which are manipulated by the key—or with a paperclip and a little work. Here's how.

STEP 1 Grab a sizeable paperclip with a thick gauge to it, as it will need some serious backbone. Unbend the paperclip's end to give you enough length and leverage to work with.

STEP 2 Have a look at your cuffs: You might see a gap near where the cuff locks into itself; if you can insert the paperclip into that gap, you can shim the cuff, using the paperclip to hold down the lock-bar holding the cuff's teeth in place, then just pull the cuff open. If you've only got a keyhole to work with, it's time for the next step.

STEP 3 Insert the paperclip's end vertically into the keyhole, then bend it to form an L-shape. Remove the paperclip—then reinsert it into the notch of the keyhole, bent part facing away from the center, and give it a careful but firm twist counter-clockwise first. You should feel the paperclip bump into the double lock bar, which keeps the cuffs from ratcheting too tight. With a little work, you may even feel a click as it gives.

STEP 4 Now, turn the paperclip clockwise, and this time, you'll feel it bump into the single lock bar that keeps the swiveling half of the cuff closed. With a little work, you should be able to disengage the single-lock and remove the cuffs. (If you have to confront your captor, you're gonna have to find something a bit sturdier than a paperclip, though.)

002 LOCK PICKING
HAIRPIN + PAPERCLIP

Locks are a social contract in physical form: "Don't touch my stuff; I won't touch yours." That said, sometimes, you just need to pick a lock. Usually a key moves a mismatched series of pins up and into a set of channels all at the same depth, letting a tumbler turn and open the lock. Picking a lock means substituting a tension wrench to hold the tumbler, and a pick to manually push the pins. Caught without keys (or lockpicks)? A paperclip and a hairpin are all you need!

STEP 1 Unbend a hairpin into a right-angled L-shape (A), and insert one end into the lock's opening. (Alternatively, you can use a tiny Allen wrench if it fits into the lock.)

STEP 2 Bend the very end of a paperclip into a tiny crook (B), and insert the paperclip into the lock above the hairpin.

STEP 3 Apply light pressure on the hairpin to hold the pins in place with the tumbler as you work on them.

STEP 4 Engage the pins in the lock by tilting the paperclip back and up, moving in a circular motion (in, up, back, and down) (C), and increase pressure on the hairpin a little each time. If raking the pins doesn't work, go one by one by inserting the paperclip until it bumps into a pin, then try to catch the pin on the end of the paperclip and push it into place, repeating with each pin until the lock opens.

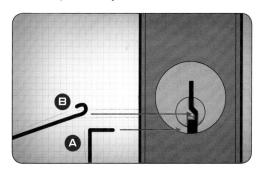

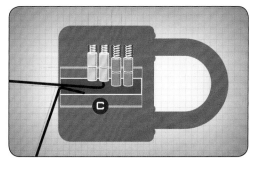

003 BUMP KEY

KEY + SAK METAL FILE

Newton's Cradle (better known as "that one executive desktop toy with the clicking steel balls") shows how kinetic energy transfers through solid objects; a steel ball impacting the row at one end transfers kinetic energy through the others, sending the last ball at the far end swinging away. Just like those neighboring steel bearings, the pins in a lock's tumbler match a set of spring-loaded driver pins further inside the lock. Most keys are cut into peaks and valleys to fit against the pins inside the tumbler, pushing them into place to turn the lock. A bump key, meanwhile, can open any lock it fits into; an impact on this key can "bump" the key pins, which in turn bump the driver pins out of the tumbler.

STEP 1 Find a spare key or key blank to match the lock you wish to open. Use a small file to cut a set of four short jagged peaks of roughly equal length and size, with one higher peak at the end of the key. Each key or blank will only fit the type of lock it's made for, but the short teeth let the driver pins stay fully pressed against the tumbler pins.

STEP 2 Insert the key into the lock fully, then very slowly draw it back until you hear one or two clicks as the bigger peak at the end of the key moves over the deepest pins.

STEP 3 Apply tension on the key as if trying to turn it in the lock, then give it a firm tap to drive it into the lock fully.

STEP 4 Repeat Steps 2 and 3 as necessary, and with some work (and assuming you're not dealing with an anti-bump lock) the bump key will turn the lock.

004 ELECTRIC LOCKPICK

ELECTRIC TOOTHBRUSH + BATTERY

As mentioned before, most locks rely on the same principle: A key is inserted into the lock, where it engages a set of pins in order to release the lock's tumbler and open it up. This means lockpicking also relies on those same ideas, whether you're picking the lock by hand, or speeding up the process with a little power—in this case, thanks to an electric toothbrush. Reusable ones are easiest, but this also works with the right kind of disposable model. It lacks the fine engineering of a genuine electric pick, but practice makes up for it, and you'll get results whether you're breaking into a notorious criminal's mansion or you just can't find the key to your favorite padlock.

STEP 1 Pull the head off of an electric toothbrush to reveal the end of the metal tip inside (A) leading to the mini motor in the handle. Cut away the neck down to the handle, exposing as much of the metal tip as possible.

STEP 2 To give this device some extra power, open the handle and remove the AA or AAA battery, then wire the terminals of a 9-volt battery (B) to the contacts inside the handle.

STEP 3 To use your new power lockpick, insert the tip of the toothbrush as with a handheld pick, along with a tension wrench (see item 002).

STEP 4 Apply mild tension on the wrench, turn on the toothbrush, and begin working it around in the lock the same with a pick. Instead of having to manually pick the pins, the metal tip's vibration does the work; once all pins are engaged, turn the tension wrench to open the lock.

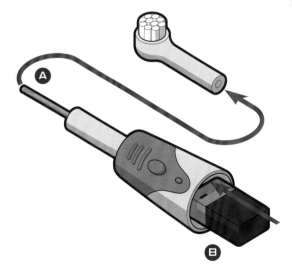

◉ ESSENTIAL KNOTS

Whether you're in the middle of a covert field op or on a relaxing camping trip, knots can be some of the most important tools in anyone's skillset. Just like any tool, using the right one for the job at hand can spell the difference between success and failure. And if you happen to be hanging from a rope twenty stories up, failure can be really, really messy.

OVERHAND KNOT

There are dozens of knots you might tie, but most are minor variations of a few essentials. The classic case of this is the overhand knot, a simple way to tie a rope or line around and through itself. Good for secure knots that are hard to untie. When used at the end of a line to keep it in place, it's called a stopper knot.

SLIPKNOT

Includes a loop that allows it to be easily untied, even one-handed.

USED FOR Animal snares, temporary restraints.

OVERHAND LOOP

Creates a sturdy loop anywhere along a length of rope.

USED FOR Attaching other ropes, or objects such as clips or carabiners.

FISHERMAN'S KNOT

Ties two ropes' ends around each other with an overhand knot in each.

USED FOR Securely joining two ropes or lines, such as climbing ropes or fishing line.

WATER KNOT

For joining webbing strips rather than rope.

USED FOR Climbing and caving.

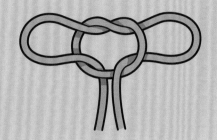

TOM FOOL'S KNOT

Overhand knot made of two bights (arches or U-shapes); fast to tie and tighten.

USED FOR Quick and easy wrist or ankle cuffs.

HONDA KNOT

Made of nothing but overhand and stopper knots.

USED FOR Making a lariat or lasso.

FIGURE EIGHT

A more complex variant of an overhand knot, the figure eight is another useful stopper knot, easily tied by making a bight, twisting it twice, and passing one end through the bight. It can be as secure as a simple overhand, but is somewhat larger and thus a bigger stopper, and a little more easily undone if it jams under a load.

005 ENVELOPE ACCESS

ENVELOPE + HEAT + COLD

Under normal circumstances, opening someone else's mail is likely to be a felony—not to mention a little nosy. But just in case you really need to get into an envelope, and don't want to cut it open or otherwise damage it, here's how. The glue that makes up the seal on an envelope isn't necessarily permanent; here are a few ways to get around it—while leaving it intact.

STEAM IT Fill a kettle or pot with water and set it to boil. Hold the envelope in the steam to let it soften the adhesive for about 15 seconds at a time so the paper doesn't get wrinkled or sodden. Apply light pressure constantly on the flap as it peels up, but don't pull or tear. It will eventually come free; you'll just have to be patient. After it's opened and cooled off, you can steam the adhesive seam again, and then seal the envelope once more.

IRON IT Set a clothes iron on medium-low, and gently run it over the back of the envelope; it should gradually melt the adhesive. This takes a little time, so don't hurry it or you'll risk scorching the paper. Once softened, use the edge of a dull knife (a sharp one can damage the envelope) to gently open it; just as with the steam method, you can moisten and seal the envelope after opening it.

FREEZE IT This takes the longest, but doesn't require heat. Slip the envelope into a plastic bag, pressing out as much air as possible, then put it in a freezer for a few hours. Afterward, you should be able to break the seal on the adhesive, using a flat, dull blade or a letter opener, without tearing the paper. Once the glue and paper warms up again, you'll be able to re-seal the envelope.

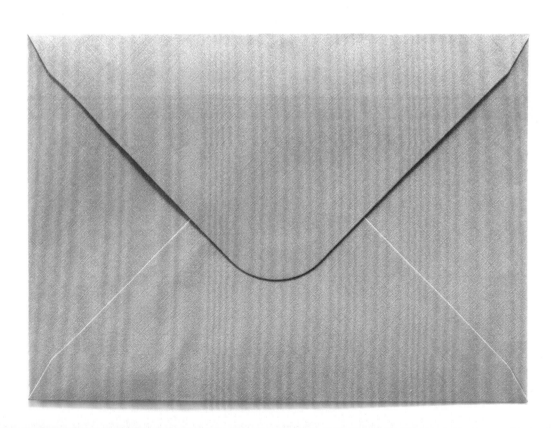

006 TUBULAR LOCK PICK
TUBULAR LOCK + PEN

Invented in the 1960s, a tubular lock is a popular model for bike locks, and uses a special key to fit its ring-shaped opening. But if you're facing one and lack a key, specialized picks, or other means, there's no need to shoot the thing open. (That almost never works anyway.) You could drill the tumblers out . . . if you just happen to have a hole-saw bit that fits the opening and don't mind attracting attention with a lot of metal-grinding noise. The good news: Tubular locks are roughly the same diameter as a ballpoint pen—or a 9mm shell casing from that gun you won't be shooting the lock with (see item 129)—so you might be able to open the way after all.

STEP 1 Grab your pen tube or bullet casing (after emptying either), and fit it into the cylinder of the lock.

STEP 2 Press down firmly, maintaining pressure as you slowly turn your 'pick' and the lock with it.

STEP 3 Tubular locks use between 7 and 10 pins, and they all need to be engaged to open the lock; with a little effort and luck, you'll eventually force the pins down, and the lock will click open.

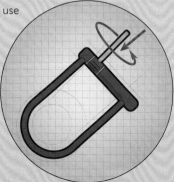

BATTERING RAM
MARBLE BUST + ROPE

If efforts in picking the lock or kicking down the door (see item 002–004 and 008) are unsuccessful, then it's time to break out the big guns for a really dramatic entrance. A SWAT team battering ram weighs about 30 pounds (14 kg) for a one-person model; 40 pounds (18 kg) for a two-person. A classical marble bust in a villain's lair? Up to a hundred pounds (45 kg), give or take!

STEP 1 Harness your would-be battering ram; marble is heavy, and handholds will make door-busting a lot easier. Tie a few lengths of rope from a nearby drape—and maybe your partner's cummerbund for good measure—around it. A Killick Hitch (see Essential Knots, Chapter 2) is a good start.

STEP 2 Get your ram off the ground to about mid-door height by taking hold of those ropes and lifting the weight together. If they're long enough and you have something to hang them from (like a heavy-duty chandelier hook), toss the rope over it and then hoist the statue to the right height.

STEP 3 Take aim at the door, focusing your efforts just next to the lock where it's most vulnerable. A very heavy door struck in the wrong place can lead to a broken ram (or at least no effect); A lightweight door means you might just bash a hole in it instead, and maybe even get the ram stuck!

STEP 4 Pull back the ram, and then swing! You're there mostly to guide the ram, but it doesn't hurt to add some of your own effort, rotating your body into the push to add more force. This might result in broken statuary, but a heavy, solid marble bust, even minus its head, is still a wrecking ball for most doors!

008 DOOR BUSTING
FEET + FORCE

If you're short on a true battering ram (or even a marble bust), you still have options. If a locked door opens toward you, for example, you can try removing its hinge pins. If it opens the other way, and if you're out of proper door-breaching tools, lockpicks, or even a credit card, you can still use the faster, way cooler approach beloved of strong-arm criminals and D&D gamers, not to mention Jack Dalton: breaking it down yourself. Naturally, this mostly works on wooden doors; for heavy steel doors and other serious portals, consider alternatives like thermite (see item 012).

SQUARE UP Throwing yourself at a door shoulder-first may look dramatic, but it's not the best technique. In fact, you're much more likely to bruise yourself, dislocate your shoulder, or worse. You shouldn't try jumping or running at it either, since you risk injury by losing your balance.

Instead, plant your non-kicking foot squarely on the ground, and lean forward a little so your weight goes fully into the kick when it's time.

KICK IT IN Aim your foot next to the doorknob or lock, instead of the mechanism itself. Raise your leg, draw back, and take a deep breath. Then, deliver a straight kick as you exhale, driving all the explosive force you can muster and connecting solidly with your heel.

FOLLOW THROUGH Your leg should be almost fully extended when the kick lands, as if you're trying to kick through the door instead of just its surface, for maximum force. It may take multiple blows, especially if you're putting the boot to a heavy door with a sturdy lock, but persist. You'll soon be rewarded with a broken door flying open on its hinges!

THE SCIENCE BEHIND
FLUORESCENCE

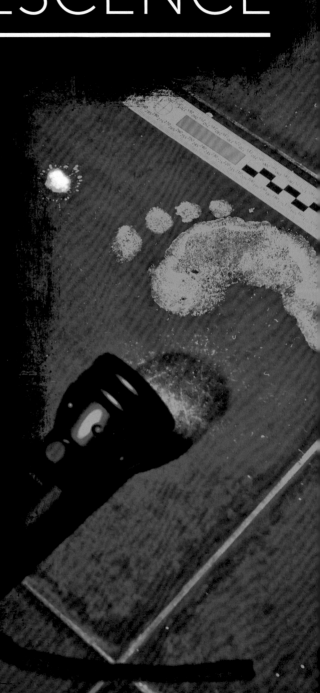

All matter is made of atoms and molecules in constant motion, vibrating with energy. For example, this is where we get heat from; the flame on a gas stove puts energy into a metal pan whose molecules, having absorbed that energy, are vibrating with it, and shed it again in the form of heat (which is why you can cook whatever is in the pan, and also why you can burn yourself on it if you're not careful).

This property also applies to other forms of energy, such as light. We see colors because various objects absorb every color except what is reflected. And, instead of simply reflecting light, certain objects will give off more energy when they're stimulated by certain types of light—this property is known as fluorescence.

The most obvious example of this is ultraviolet (UV) or "black" light interacting with day-glow items such as highlighter markers and their ink. Ultraviolet waves are higher on the electromagnetic spectrum than visible light (also known as "white" light), and visible light is higher in frequency than infrared (IR)—commonly felt as heat, even if it's unseen. Ultraviolet light also transmits more energy than visible light or infrared. When exposed to UV, the fluorescent item absorbs more energy, thus boosting its molecules' vibration, and raising them from their "ground state." Now, all that energy has to go somewhere in order for those molecules in that fluorescent-colored substance to return to their non-excited ground state, and so they give it off in the form of—you guessed it—light!

009 UV PASS FILTER

MARKER + TAPE + DISKETTE

The human eye can only see within the visible range, but black lights—a staple of nightclubs, dorm rooms, and psychedelic posters everywhere—add some extra illumination. With your cell phone and a few simple parts, you can make your own by filtering the light from the flashlight's LED. You won't have as much illumination as if it were ultraviolet and unfiltered, and certain substances that only glow under true UV won't react to this light, but you should be able to enhance certain materials like highlighter markers.

TAPE IT UP Lay three strips of clear tape over your phone's LED, each with a layer of permanent marker ink: two dark blue layers and one dark purple. Together, these will create a filter that only allows light close to the ultraviolet range to shine through, getting a bright phosphorescent reaction.

GET IT ON DISK Floppy disks and diskettes are made of a plastic material covered in a thin metallic layer that can filter out certain types of light depending on the coating (see item 128). Open a disk's casing and extract the disk inside. Hold it up against or tape it to your phone's LED; if the coating is the right type, you'll get similar results as with layers of tape.

010 INTRUDER DETECTION

DOORMAT + UV LIGHT

The human eye can see in the visible spectrum, where light energy is seen from red to violet, roughly between 380 and 740 nanometers. Above this range is infrared—heat energy—and below it is ultraviolet; although we can't see outside the visible spectrum, we can still make use of its properties.

For example, if you're concerned you've been getting unexpected visitors at home, your front doormat and an ultraviolet light bulb can be a simple means of telling if you should expect company. Give your doormat a light dusting of a powdered UV-reactive material that's barely visible under regular light such as ground turmeric, or powdered detergent or bleach, and set it out carefully. Check later on by sweeping an ultraviolet light over the mat (see item 009). If you've had anyone come by, you'll see a blank spot in the shape of a footprint where their shoe disturbed and picked up the powder on your doormat.

011 ACID INGRESS

ACID + CONCRETE

Muriatic acid is a form of good old hydrochloric acid (HCl) suspended in water at up to about 30% concentration—but even then, it's a powerful corrosive. Small amounts etch concrete; large amounts eat through it instead. With enough acid, you can burn a tunnel through a wall—like the one under that heavily-guarded compound you're looking to sneak into.

GEAR UP Glass containers hold most acids safely, but high-density polyethylene (HDPE) is shatter-proof and acid-resistant, so it's often used instead. You'll need HDPE pump-pressure sprayers, tubing, and at least one big barrel of acid (the higher concentration, the better) to make a human-sized hole in a thick concrete wall.

DIG IN Along with water, and aggregates such as gravel or sand, concrete includes cement—a combination of alkaline calcium-bearing minerals that bind the aggregate together. When it reacts with acid, the bonds in those calciferous minerals dissolve as some of the chlorine binds to them, leaving a brittle greenish gunk that easily breaks away. Be patient; this will take some time and a lot of scraping. (Luckily, HDPE also makes for good solid hand tools!)

STAY SAFE Hydrochloric acid is highly dangerous; it might not instantly burn through things like movie acid, but even its vapors can burn your skin, eyes, and lungs. A sealed hazmat suit is a bare minimum for safety. Hydrogen gas is a major byproduct, so invest in ventilation: A single spark in a confined space can be explosive even without oxygen, since chlorine gas, the other half of HCl, acts as an oxidizer. (See The Science of Explosions, in Chapter 5.)

012 THERMITE

IRON + ALUMINUM + HEAT

Sometimes, a paperclip just won't be enough to get you in, such as when facing an armored van's metal doors. Welding torches are bulky and shaped charges are noisy, but there's something almost as hot as the first and a lot quieter than the second: Thermite, a finely-powdered combination of a metal oxide and another metal. Its reaction easily welds metal objects together, or melts right through them (and almost anything else nearby!).

START WITH IRON Rust makes up about 75% of a basic thermite mix: Red (Fe_2O_3) or black (Fe_3O_4) iron oxide is found in rusted iron or jeweler's rouge polishing dust; black iron oxide is also a product of burning steel wool (see Don't Get Caught Without Fire, Chapter 5).

ADD ALUMINUM The other 25% of thermite is found in soda cans, tinfoil, paints, and dyes. Aside from buying powdered aluminum or hand-shredding it, you make it with a coffee grinder—carefully. The powder can ignite if overheated so grind foil shreds in bursts, pausing to let it cool.

BIND IT TOGETHER Mixed thoroughly but carefully, thermite can be stored in a sealed container in a cool, dry location as-is, or it can be made into a putty. Instead of a 3:1 ratio, you'll need a 3:2:2 weight ratio of rust, aluminum, and calcium sulfate ($CaSO_4$), also known as gypsum or Plaster of Paris—a powerful oxidizer in its own right. Add enough water to mix everything together and you'll have a wet putty that hardens and dries as it cures.

BRING THE HEAT Thermite gets a kickstart from a powerful source source of heat such as magnesium, the main active ingredient in sparklers and road flares, or even some hypergolic mixtures such as glycerine and potassium permanganate (see Don't Get Caught Without Fire). But once ignited, a chemical reaction strips the oxygen from the iron, and creates even more heat as the metals melt—up to 4,500 °F (2,480 °C), enough heat to put a hole in an engine block! Stand back and shield your eyes: thermite also puts out UV light that can damage your vision (see item 128).

013 DOOR BREACHING BALLISTA

BED FRAME + CHAIR + EXTENSION CORD

Crossbows have been around for millennia, for good reason: they store even more kinetic energy than a hand-drawn bow, and while slower to load, they're easier to wield. This power means, if you build a big enough crossbow—called a ballista—you can even bust a door if you launch something heavy at it. And if, for example, you're trapped behind a heavy steel door in a fallout shelter, short on welding tools, out of thermite, and with no battering ram, you've got some time. (As with any weapon, don't point this at anything you don't intend to destroy.)

YOU'LL NEED

- Metal chair
- Metal bed frame parts
- Extension cord
- Folding steel table legs
- Heavy-duty extension springs
- Steel soup can
- Stainless steel fork
- Steel oxygen tank

STEP 1 Cut the bars out of the chair back, then lash the headboard and rails to the chair to make your frame.

STEP 2 Start building the lath: Using the extension cord, lash two table legs to the top of the headboard by their guide pins so that they swivel freely.

STEP 3 Hook an extension spring to the top of each table leg and lash it to the bottom of the headboard near the side rails.

STEP 4 Twist a few lengths of extension cord together to make a bowstring, then tie it in catspaws (see Essential Knots, Chapter 5) to the ends of the table legs. Tie the cord off in square knots (see Essential Knots, Chapter 2).

STEP 5 For a crank, punch two small parallel slits in the bottom of a steel soup can, and insert a steel fork by its middle tines; set this on the leg at the foot of your ballista frame.

STEP 6 Tie electrical cord around the end of the bed frame middle leg support, and then tie the other end around the crank.

STEP 7 Hook the bracket end of the leg support into the bowstring, and load your ballista with an empty steel oxygen tank. Turn the crank to draw the string back.

STEP 8 Once it's loaded and cocked, clear your firing path. Take aim, release the crank, and watch as your oxygen tank takes flight!

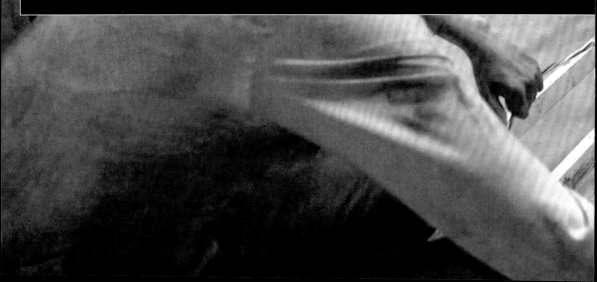

COULD I DO THAT?!

Air pressure in our atmosphere doesn't just mean air pressing down on us thanks to gravity; air has its own pressure on literally all sides of an object since it is matter, and thus has mass. A vacuum, meanwhile, is the absence of mass inside a given volume; anything exposed to it tries to replace the emptiness. Suction lowers the pressure between two surfaces, creating a partial vacuum, while the remaining air outside continues to provide pressure. As long as you have a strong enough vacuum effect holding the two objects together, the force used on one can pull the other along with it. With enough suction on a surface as small as the mouth of a plastic cup, you could easily lift half the weight of an average human being.

Equipped with a pair of cordless vacuum cleaners, MacGyver was able to climb the glass exterior of a high-rise, holding a set of suction cups attached to the ends of the vacuum hoses and pulling himself up hand over hand. To do this, you'd need working vacuum cleaners that are fully charged; you'd have to then add a set of very large suction cups or other surfaces with a good edge seal attached to each vacuum nozzle

(it turns out that circular objects work best at providing maximum suction and minimal extra surface area), and a set of one-way valves in each suction system to release suction without turning off the vacuum.

Window washer and repair teams regularly work outside high-rise buildings; although they mainly use scaffolding and other equipment to ascend and descend, suction cups are part of their equipment for climbing and for handling glass. Meanwhile, "Spider Dan" Goodwin, who climbed the Sears Tower in Chicago in 1981, or Steven Rogata, who scaled Trump Tower in 2016, used nothing more than a set of heavy-duty suction cups and some minimal climbing equipment. Professional climber Sierra Blair-Coyle demonstrated the power of suction by scaling a 33-story building in South Korea, also in 2016, using a vacuum-cleaner mechanism very similar to MacGyver's.

So, could you do this? You could indeed—but we can't stress enough that it would be very risky, especially if you're not a trained professional climber. We hope you're not afraid of heights!

014 SUCTION CLIMBER

VACUUM CLEANER + METAL TRAY

Suction can come from passive sources, like rubber cups with handles, or from active ones such as vacuum cleaners. Both can be used to hold things up, but the latter can provide a lot more power. Here's how to use it to your advantage in a climb, even if you're not clinging to the windows of a high-rise. For added safety, consider using a Swiss Seat (see item 063) or climbing harness attached to a belaying line.

YOU'LL NEED

- Cordless vacuum cleaner
- Large metal champagne tray or baking pan
- 1-inch (2.5 cm) soft rubber tubing
- Heavy-duty rubber cement or silicone adhesive
- Door pull handle with screws
- Button bleeder valve
- Rope

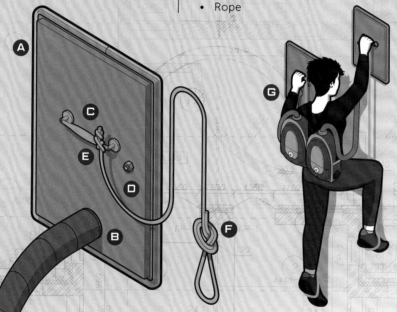

STEP 1 Measure tubing to fit precisely around the lip of the pan, then cut it open lengthwise and glue it in place (A).

STEP 2 Draw the outline of the vacuum's suction tube into the middle of the pan, and cut a hole to fit. Insert the end of the nozzle into the hole (B); seal the edge with duct tape or adhesive.

STEP 3 Drill a pair of holes into the pan near the suction tube, and install the handle (C).

STEP 4 Drill a hole next to the handle within reach of your thumb (D) and install the bleeder valve.

STEP 5 Tie the rope to the handle, starting with a stopper knot followed by a clove hitch (E) (see Essential Knots, Chapter 2). Tie its end into a loop big enough to fit your foot (F). Repeat steps 1 through 5 to build a second climbing device.

STEP 6 Sling your vacuums over your back, power them up, and hold the pans firmly against a wall to stick them in place.

STEP 7 Slip your feet into the loops on the ropes and step up, while holding onto the handles (G).

STEP 8 Push the button on the bleeder valve to release the suction pan, and raise your arm and leg before sticking it to the wall higher up. Continue climbing away!

015 BASIC SECURITY BYPASS

STEALTH + MAGNET + BLANKET

Most security systems rely on a few simple components. Unless you're able to hack into network like Riley and shut it down or bypass it, you'll have to deal with at least one security measure in person. Here are a few methods you potentially can use to bypass them, or to test your own home's protections.

CAMERAS Ultra-wide-angle dome cameras can span up to 360 degrees while sacrificing a clear image, but the average wide-angle security camera covers about an 80-degree field of view with a much less distorted picture. Your best bet is to just stay clear of their sight; the best approach, ironically, is to remain very close to the camera, in order to keep just outside of its field of view. You can also blind one with tape, mud, or cloth—which eventually will be discovered—or with light (see item 098).

SENSORS Alarmed doors and windows often use small magnetic sensors—one on the frame and another on the door or window itself. When they're moved apart, the alarm is tripped. If the magnet is reachable, tape another small magnet (such as one from your refrigerator) to the frame-side sensor, or remove the sensor from the door and tape it to its counterpart.

MOTION DETECTORS Infrared, optical, radio, sound, and other sensors exist along with cameras, but treat them the same: if you can see them, try to stay outside their range. Move slowly and quietly if you have to cross them. You can even use a sheet or blanket with some sensors, which will treat a broad flat surface as a wall. If you suspect infrared sensors, and you can turn up the heat to human body temperature, you might be hidden against the background.

016 HIDDEN DOOR DETECTION

CANDLE + WATER + UV LIGHT

Before you can pick a door's lock (see items 002–004) or even break through it (for more on that, see items 007–008), sometimes you have to find it first. Every entrance and exit might be clearly marked in an airplane or movie theater, but you're out of luck in plenty of other places. Want to find your way out of an escape room, or into a mad bomber's secret lair? Here are some tips.

SCAN THE SURROUNDINGS

Try knocking on surfaces to check for hidden spaces, or feel for changes in temperature: both could be clues to hidden passages or mechanisms. Anything moveable, from a wall sconce to a leatherbound book on a shelf, could be a switch for a hidden door. You won't find every portal in a wall, either; sometimes the floor or ceiling itself hides a secret exit. You might even have multiple layers of stealth to contend with, like a table and chair on a rug over a thin wood panel hiding a disguised hatchway.

CHECK FOR LEAKS

Unless it's fully sealed, every doorway has a small gap under or around it. Differences in temperature and air pressure (especially in a rambling old mansion's hidden passages, or catacombs under the streets of a city) mean drafts can blow through those gaps. A flickering candle or lighter flame, or a disturbed wisp of smoke can show the way. Air currents are only one way; you can also pour some water onto the floor, watch where it goes, and listen for any dripping through hatch seams to a hidden room below.

ENHANCE YOUR SENSES

Not all hidden doors or portals will have a means of access you can spot, but even then, there are still clues to seek, and there's no reason not to use any means available to improve the odds of detection. For example, magnetically locked doors can still give off an electromagnetic field that will disturb a compass (see item 036), while secret markings showing the way can be written in fluorescent "invisible ink" that glows brightly under ultraviolet light (see The Science of Phosphorescence, and items 009–010).

017 ROPE BINDING ESCAPOLOGY

Chains, handcuffs, zip ties, duct tape, and of course ropes all see use as ways of keeping people from getting very far. If you or someone else is bound by any of the former items, there are ways out (see items 001–002, 004, and 018–019); for the latter, here's how to ensure your best chance at an early release if you're unable to reach your Swiss Army knife (or if you happen to be wearing a shirt without buttons—see item 021).

BE COOPERATIVE (KINDA) Let your captor tie your wrists, but keep your arms close to your sides and muscles clenched in your forearms and hands. If your torso or legs are being bound, hold your breath and flex every muscle you can.

GET SOME SLACK Once your captor finishes the ties and their attention is elsewhere, rotate your wrists together, exhale, and relax your body; You should get a little bit of slack in all your bonds as a result.

STRETCH OUT AND SWEAT Once things are a little loosened, begin working your wrists (or any other bound limbs) back and forth, around, and against each other and the rope; as you do so, the rope should stretch out a little. As an added bonus, you're likely to perspire in this kind of situation—and the sweat will help reduce friction between the ropes and you.

GIVE IT ALL YOUR BITE If you can get your hands up to your face, you can also use your teeth to help work loose the bindings and pick at any troublesome knots. Once your ties are loose enough to free your hands, the rest will follow!

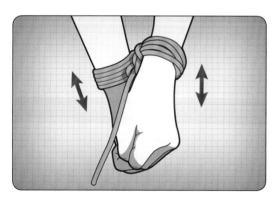

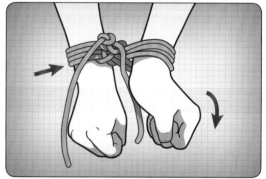

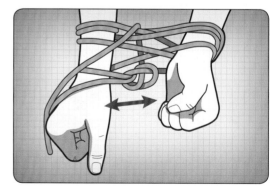

018 ZIP TIE BREAKOUT

ZIP TIES + TECHNIQUE

Whether as part of the plan or because an adversary got the drop on you, you're now in someone else's clutches—and worse still, you're cuffed (and if you are in real handcuffs, see item 001). Zip ties are a common means of restraint since they're quickly and easily deployed. But this also means they can be quickly and easily escaped. Here are several ways to free yourself.

DECEPTION If you can do so before being tied, keep your fists close together horizontally, muscles clenched much as possible, and flare your elbows out. Then after the tie is on, relax and rotate your palms together to give yourself a little more space to work with, and try to wriggle out.

TOOLS The ratchet mechanism on zip ties can be foiled if you have something small and rigid to lever it off the plastic strip. Virtually any tool in a Swiss Army knife can do the trick, but even the corner of a credit card or the tip of a pen could work.

FRICTION Even a simple cord can saw through zip ties. Slip a shoelace or bootlace around the tie, and pull it back and forth rapidly, concentrating on one spot. Within several seconds, the pressure and friction will cut through the plastic.

HEAT Melting plastic isn't too hard, so this escape is simple: Find a small candle or lighter flame, or a hot wire like one in a heating element or on a coil stove, will quickly melt through the tie. (Use caution; you might singe yourself in the bargain.)

FORCE Tighten (yes, tighten) the cuffs as much as you can, then lift your arms up, hands overhead and elbows out past hips. Bring your arms down hard and fast while pulling your hands apart to snap the ties. Bonus: This even works with duct-tape bindings!

019 DUCT TAPE LIBERATION

DUCT TAPE + FORCE + SPEED

Duct tape obviously has a lot of uses (see Don't Get Caught Without Duct Tape, Chapter 4), and one of the most well-known is a quick, convenient restraint. Hobbled and bound by duct tape bindings? Here's how to get free fast.

STEP 1 Be compliant and hold your hands out together to be bound and keep your feet together; you need your wrists and ankles to be as close together as possible.

STEP 2 Once unobserved, raise your hands over your head, and swing your arms down hard and fast, to slam them elbows-first against the sides of your ribcage.

STEP 3 Follow through on the downward swing, and as your elbows flare outward, the sudden impact and shear force should tear through the tape.

STEP 4 Next, for your leg bindings, put your hands together, palms facing each other, and slide them between your knees.

STEP 5 Force your hands and forearms down together between your knees and down the length of your shins; the sudden force should likewise split the tape.

020 QUICKSAND EVASION

CAUTION + PATIENCE + POLE

Quicksand is formed when sand, silt, or other fine-grain material is saturated with water. It's a non-Newtonian fluid—that is, it looks solid when stable, until pressure changes or agitation cause it to liquefy again. In other words, it's liquid soil that becomes more fluid when you try to walk into (or out of) it. Patches of quicksand usually aren't very deep, and drowning doesn't happen often, but they can be extremely difficult to escape, and quicksand fatalities still occur from dehydration, exposure, or suffocation.

KNOW WHAT TO AVOID Quicksand is found mostly in forests or beaches, but can be pretty much anywhere you can mix fine granular soil and water. Keep an eye out for unusually wet, muddy, or rippled-looking patches of ground, especially on sand; in a forested area, the surface may be obscured by dead leaves and other debris. Prodding the ground ahead of you with a walking stick is an easy early-detection method. Once you

begin walking across quicksand, you'll find out quickly as it gives way and begins to pull you in deeper, especially if you struggle too much and displace the quicksand faster as it liquefies.

KNOW HOW TO GET OUT If you find yourself slogging through quicksand, stop moving immediately. You might sink a little bit, but most patches are only about waist-deep—which is still more than enough to trap you if you struggle further. If you have a non-stuck buddy with you, have them try to pull you out, so long as they're not in it as well. Try laying back, since more surface area atop the quicksand means more buoyancy, and if you have a walking stick or pole (you did bring one, right?) put it under your hips or the small of your back as another support. From here, you can pull your limbs free, but you'll have to go slowly; quicksand doesn't flow back into gaps very rapidly, and a vacuum effect in the open space will fight back as well.

021 MINIATURE BLADE

BUTTON + FRICTION

Escaping rope ties is done easiest if you have a knife. Usually, though, when the bad guy wants to make sure you're not going to escape or fight back, he'll make sure you have no knives on you. Still, if you have something small and lightweight within reach—like a button—you might just be out of those ropes before too long.

STEP 1 Pull the largest button you can reach off of your shirt. Sometimes this requires a bit of struggling to reach one, but once you pull it off, you'll be halfway there.

STEP 2 Hold this button tightly between thumb and forefinger, because your life might depend on it, and then rub it steadily back and forth at a consistent angle on something solid (like the pavement under you) or try to break off part of the button in a gap between the parts of the chair you're tied to.

STEP 3 Once you have a reasonably sharp edge (this tiny blade won't be razor-sharp, but "sharp enough") curl your hand holding the button to draw the edge against the ropes. Focus on one spot, and saw back and forth, applying steady pressure. This is going to take some time: you have something about the size of an Exacto knife but not as sharp, so you'll wear through the fibers of the rope just as much as you cut them, but you'll get free eventually—a distraction from a partner helps, if you're being watched or interrogated.

022 MAXIMUM SECURITY BREAKOUT

EXPLOSIVES + CRYOGENIC FLUID + MISDIRECTION

Busting out of prison is no easy feat, even with improvised explosives and bar-breaking cryogenics at your disposal (see items 023 and 024). Unless you really want to end up explaining to the warden why you needed to free the drug kingpin sharing your cell, you should be using every means possible.

MAKE SOME NOISE If you have any allies on the inside—maybe even the drug kingpin sharing your cell—see if they can trigger a riot as a distraction. (Prison guards generally take a dim view of rowdy prisoners brawling and throwing flaming objects around.)

CONFUSE COMMUNICATIONS Got hold of a radio? Use it to call guards to a location of your choice, and clear them out of your path. Even if it doesn't work, the ensuing confusion over who's really on the radio can still help you.

MISLEAD PURSUERS Just because you're taking an escape route doesn't mean you can't make people think that you're taking another. Hang a rope and grappling hook (see item 028) on a ledge, set up a ladder leading onto a roof, or toss a spare jumpsuit or blanket over a barbed-wire or razor-wire fence (see item 026) that you won't be climbing anyway. While they're investigating, you'll be in the wind.

CRYOGENIC FLUID

DRY ICE + ALCOHOL

A cryogenic fluid is a substance with an extremely low freezing point—liquid nitrogen is the most well known. If you need to make something extremely cold, you can substitute with just two more easily-found materials: dry ice, and rubbing alcohol.

CO2 fire extinguishers are great for producing a cloud of dry ice if you spray one into a closed container (like a large trash can), but solid ice chips are even better. Put your dry ice chips into a sturdy plastic container, and add enough rubbing alcohol to fully saturate the ice; highest alcohol content is best, such as 99% isopropyl. This mix will be extremely cold, around -110°F (-79°C) even as a liquid, thanks to the alcohol. It'll stick to most anything: skin, broom bristles, and those old iron prison bars in your way. They'll change from flexible to brittle at about 0°F (-17°C), and will crack with sharp blows or forceful leverage.

024 EXPLOSIVE JAILBREAK

BATTERY + SALT WATER

"Electrolysis" is a term for chemical change in a liquid caused by an electric current. It's used in submarines where water is broken down into hydrogen and oxygen; the latter of those two is really important if the sub crews want to keep breathing when they're deep underwater. The former, hydrogen, is a highly flammable gas, great for lifting zeppelins in the 1930s—and escaping a jail cell when you're locked up with a notorious drug lord. Here's how it works.

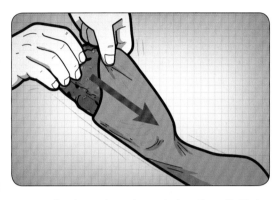

STEP 1 Ready an electrolyte solution. Pure distilled water is a poor conductor, but salt dissolves into sodium and chloride ions in water, which conduct electricity very well. Low on salt packets? Stuff a sock full of prison rations or nutraloaf, and soak it in water.

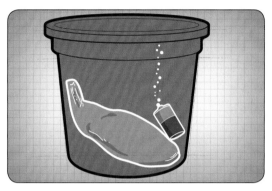

STEP 2 Add a power source. A large, fully-charged battery from a guard's radio works wonderfully if you submerge the leads (or maybe the whole thing). A tiny stream of bubbles will form on the terminals as the water is electrolysed into hydrogen and oxygen.

STEP 3 Prepare for ignition. For this jailbreak, you will need lots of hydrogen, which means a lot of water, salt, battery power, and plenty of patience while enough gas forms. Pass the time by prying open the ceiling light fixture, stripping two of the wires, and then tying a string to reach the wires from the floor.

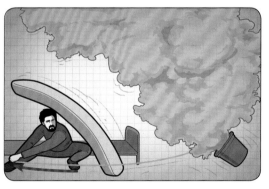

STEP 4 Take cover, preferably under something sizeable and padded, like the mattress on your prison cot (see item 079 for more) and then pull the string to bring the wires together. The spark will ignite the hydrogen cloud, and the explosion will definitely attract some attention—if the fire alarm doesn't first—so once your cell is breached, get moving!

025 BRICK WALL CLIMBING

BRICK WALL + REBAR

Brick-and-mortar construction is an ages-old favorite: It's easily laid down, durable—and really difficult to climb if well built. But you don't need to be Spider-Man or a parkour practitioner to get up a brick wall. Here's how to make that wall a walk (or climb) in the park.

PLAN YOUR PATH Before beginning, have a look at where you want to go, from both the bottom up, and from your topside destination down. You won't get anywhere if you're halfway up the wall and run out of climbing route.

USE ALL YOUR LIMBS Skilled climbers, whether the human or the mountain-goat variety, know to use every limb possible to maintain purchase. Keep three points of contact if you can for best stability, using the fourth limb to reach your next contact point, before moving another limb to the next point.

BE A MOUNTAINEER Brick walls aren't exactly like icefalls or rock faces, but mortar still chips away like soft rock or ice. Even without high-tech climbing shoes, you can still use objects like scavenged sections of rebar for pitons or a climbing axe, strapped to your soles as crampons, or perhaps a grappling hook (see item 028).

SEEK EVERY ADVANTAGE Any good point is fair game, from a slightly protruding brick or pipe to the tiniest rough edge or narrow divot in the mortar. Just be sure it'll hold you up by gradually applying more of your weight before trusting it fully—older walls have more available climbing points, but can also crumble more readily.

026 BARBED WIRE CROSSING
BARBED WIRE FENCE + PADDING

Barbed wire was first invented as a way to keep cattle from wandering, but quickly found use as fortifications in trench warfare and private-property lines. You can cut your way through a barbed-wire fence with the right tools, or dig underneath it if you have time, but how do you get past a high wire-topped barricade if you don't want to damage property or leave evidence of your crossing?

USE PROTECTION Barbed or razor wire is meant to discourage would-be trespassers by using pain and injury, so your first order of business is to protect against that. Throw a folded blanket, an old rug or towel, a piece of heavy clothing, or even a dense heap of nearby foliage over the top of the fence. (Just don't forget to bring it with you afterward unless you want to draw attention—especially if you plan on getting out the same way.)

TAKE THE MIDDLE If the fence has old-fashioned barbed wire strung horizontally along the top of the fence, your best bet for a speedy trip over is to climb up at the midpoint between two posts. Press down the wire under the padding to lower it and make it easier to surmount.

TRY A POST If the wire is strung in loops, approach a post instead, especially in the case of razor wire on angled brackets tilted outward. Place the padding of your choice on top of the post, and then use the post's stability to help get you over.

FIND A HEIGHT BREAK One of the easiest places to cross this kind of fence is where its height changes, along with the height of the wire. You'll usually find fenceposts at height breaks, too, which will add more stability to your climb.

027 HIGH WALL ASCENSION
WALL + POLE + PRESSURE

You're at the foot of a three-story building, and with no reasonable means of entry at the ground floor. So, how do you get in? It turns out, all you need to do is overcome gravity. Sounds obvious but impossible? Not at all; as long as you have enough friction you'll be up there in no time.

Friction is what gives you traction to move. You're working against gravity the whole time your feet are moving or your car's tires are rolling, propelling you horizontally or even up a slope; geckos, meanwhile, have enough friction due to

their toes' structure that they can stick to a vertical surface instead. You're no gecko, so you need a lot of pressure and friction to walk vertically.

For example, if you plant your foot against a wall, while clutching tightly to the end of a long sturdy pole, someone else can push forward from the other end. All that pressure means friction, keeping you from slipping as you walk up the wall . . . just so long as your friends are applying pressure below and behind you the whole way. You're not afraid of heights, are you?

028 GRAPPLING HOOK

REBAR + ROPE

For climbing walls like a ninja or special-forces operator, dragging an area for landmines, or just pulling something from over there to right here, nothing beats the grappling hook—a simple apparatus of metal hooks on the end of a rope. If you don't have one ready-made, here's how you can put one together.

YOU'LL NEED

- Narrow steel pipe about 3 feet (1 m) long
- 3 lengths of rebar, about 18 inches (45 cm) each
- Natural-fiber rope

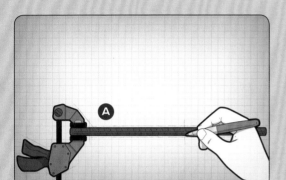

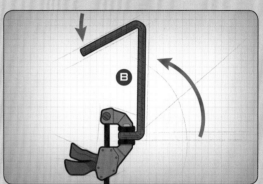

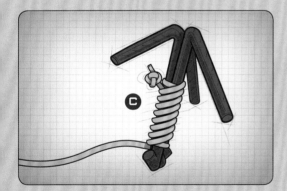

STEP 1 Clamp each rebar (A) or otherwise stabilize it, and then measure and mark each rebar about 6 inches (15 cm) from one end, and about 1 ½ inches (3.75 cm) from the other.

STEP 2 Slide a long steel pipe onto the rebar up to the markings, then use the pipe to bend each rebar at each mark (B), creating a shape like the number 7 with a hook at the bottom.

STEP 3 Bundle all of the rebars together with their hooks facing outward, and bind them together tightly with the rope (C). Start with a stopper knot just under the top hooks, and work to the bottom with clove hitches. (see Essential Knots, Chapter 2).

STEP 4 To throw your grappling hook, hold the rope a short distance under the bottom of the hook, begin spinning it underhand (D), then cast it with a snap of your wrist (E).

STEP 5 Pull steadily on the rope until the hooks grab your target and reel it in, or carefully test the hook set with your full body weight, then climb away!

TOOLS
+TECHNOLOGY

SHOCK AND AWE

There's a perfect tool for every job. And while MacGyver almost always has his signature Swiss Army knife, even the best model doesn't have a metal detector or stun gun. What if you need one of those? Just like Mac, once you understand the science behind these tools, you just might be able to rig up a DIY solution.

ELECTROSTATICS Everything around you (really, absolutely everything) has both positive and negative charges inside. The positive charges are from protons in each atom's nucleus, while the negative charges are electrons in the outer shells of an atom. You can see evidence of nature's fondness for electric charges when you pull your socks out of the drier. Due to a transfer of charge, some socks gain an excess of static and become attracted to other objects.

You can even store excess electric charge. This is exactly what MacGyver did with his improvised Leyden jar in Season 1, Episode 13. The jar is essentially made up of two materials that are electrical conductors separated by an insulator like plastic. Since electric charges can't move through the insulator, you can achieve a large build-up across the conductors. This charge can then be used for important things—like charging a phone or shocking your friend.

ELECTRIC CIRCUITS We live in a world of electric circuits, from the lights in your house to your smartphone. Even a car wouldn't work without one. If you want to understand circuits, then you'll need to consider two main ideas: voltage and current.

In metal materials (such as iron, aluminum, copper, and gold) there are free electrons that are able to move around. This makes these materials electrical conductors. But how do you get these electric charges to move

and create a current? Voltage is the answer. Think of it like a hill, and the charge as a ball. If you put a ball at the top of a hill, it will roll down just like an electric voltage will push electric charges from one area to another.

But if you want an electrical device to work, you need a be sure your contraption makes a complete circuit. The electric charges in a current don't get "used up," but they do have to make a complete round trip in order for it to do the job. If you hook a lightbulb up to a battery, you need wires going between the positive and negative terminal of the battery and the bulb. This is exactly what happens with something crazy awesome like an arc lamp where current passing from one carbon rod to the other can produce super bright light.

THE MAGIC OF MAGNETS Surely you have played with a magnet at some point. If not, go find

one right now. When a magnet is brought near some (but not all) metals, you can feel an invisible attractive force. It really feels like magic, even to a physics professor.

There are two basic ways to make a magnetic interaction. The first way seems obvious—just get a magnet with a North and South pole. You can actually find these in nature, in a phenomenon called a lodestone—it's just a magnetized piece of iron, but it's still a magnet. Other than that, you can find a permanent magnet inside of an old hard drive or in a stereo speaker. There are probably even magnets stuck on the outside of your refrigerator. Another, hard to miss, magnet is . . . the Earth! A free-floating magnet in a compass (see item 036) will interact with the Earth's magnetic field and end up pointing North.

Another way to make a magnet is with an electric current, since the moving charges inside a circuit also create an magnetic field. The electromagnetic field geneated by a single wire is not that great. But take a wire and form a bunch of loops, and you can make a powerful electromagnet (such as in item 043). The nice thing about this kind of magnet is that you can turn it on and off with an electrical switch.

GRACE UNDER PRESSURE What if you want to make your electronic tool function when it's up in the air? Maybe you want to build a hot air balloon for your smartphone or even a syringe-based animated skeleton—you know, for fun? (See items 045 and 046.) In both of cases you'll want to use the principle of pressure, which in a scientific context (as compared to the pressure Mac often finds himself under!) is defined as an applied force divided by the contact area for that force.

How about a pressure example? If you push on a wooden door with your flat hand, you can exert a significant force and nothing really happens to the wood. Now take that same force and push on the door with a nail. Since the nail has a much smaller contact area it can produce a larger pressure. This pressure is large enough to puncture the wood. Pressure matters.

Pressure is also why things float in the air or in the water. For a balloon, the atmosphere pushes in all directions. If the pressure below a balloon is larger than the pressure above, you can get a net upward force, which we call buoyancy. In the air, this pressure is usually pretty small. But if you get a large enough balloon, the buoyancy force can lift a phone, or even a human.

SWISS ARMY KNIFE

When something is referred to as the Swiss Army knife of its kind, people think versatility, durability, and ingenuity. Although it wasn't the first pocket knife with extra tools, the venerable SAK created in the late 1800s has been the most popular—and certainly the most packed with gadgets, blades, and even lighters. You don't have to bring a Wenger Giant SAK in the field (nor should you!), but here are some of the most useful tools you'll want to have.

(A) KNIFE When you need to cut something, whether it's rope keeping someone tied up, or a space blanket that needs shredding to confuse surface-to-air missiles (see item 078), you won't have to look far. A basic blade is all you need, and a Swiss Army Knife wouldn't really be called such without one.

(B) SCREWDRIVER So many things in this world are held together by screws—and luckily, a SAK has flat, Phillips, even hex driver heads. No bomb casing (or DVD player, or wall switch plate) can stand in your way.

(C) SCISSORS This option is great whether you need to snip wires in a bomb, or just trim a loose thread from your fancy tailored suit before infiltrating a high-class party.

(D) PLIERS Small nuts and bolts are another fact of modern life, and this attachment can help— and with related tasks like wire stripping, or just holding something in its jaws.

(E) AWL Poking holes in things may seem overrated, but having the ability to do so, such as when you need to turn a stick into a handle for more leverage on a small tool (see item 112), is more useful than you'd expect.

(F) SAW Both metal- and wood-cutting varieties are found in a SAK, and eventually you'll need to hack your way through something, whether it's a PVC pipe for an air raid siren (see item 091), or drywall and wood panelling hiding an explosive.

(G) TWEEZERS From pulling out a splinter to manipulating fine components in a watch to bridging the terminals in a battery and starting a survival fire (see item 038), these tiny metal grippers are perfect.

(H) MAGNIFYING GLASS Small numbers etched into something you can't read unaided? Have to start a fire? Or maybe you're facing a monkey holding a detonator, and need something shiny and distracting to trade? Look no further!

029 BLOCK AND TACKLE

ROPE + PIPE

A pulley, like all of the simple machines, is built to redirect or multiply force or speed exerted on it. The more pulleys that are used, the more force is multiplied, thus reducing the amount of energy needed to move objects. If you want to pull, drag, or lift an object—whether it's bulky furniture, a heavy safe, or your best buddy on a covert op who got stuck in a too-narrow escape tunnel—here's the basic idea.

STEP 1 Tie your rope in a fixed loop (such as with a bowline—see Essential Knots, Chapter 3) around the object (or person) that you need to move.

STEP 2 Run the rope around a nearby fixed point such as a post, or through an anchored pulley wheel.

STEP 3 Thread the rope's free end through the loop tied around the item in Step 1, or add a second pulley wheel to the loop if you have one.

STEP 4 Hold tightly to the free end of the rope, and pull! If you were just dragging the object along with no pulley, you'd have no mechanical advantage. A single pulley lets you change the direction of force with the same amount of energy exerted. But with the rope directed back to the original load, then pulled, you have a two-to-one mechanical advantage—your strength is doubled. For each loop or pulley added, between the fixed point and the object to be moved, your strength multiplies further!

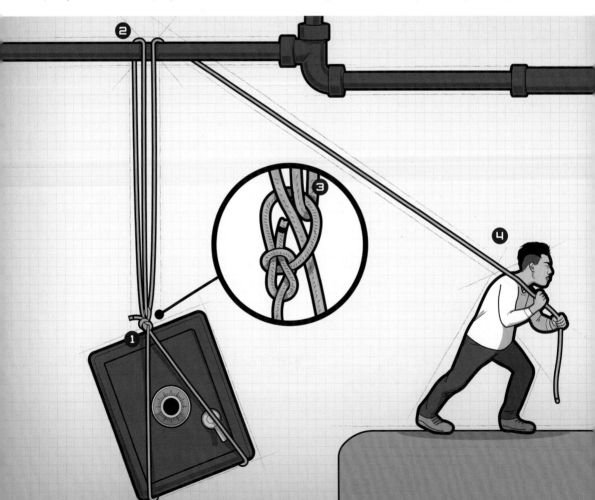

030 JACK SCREW

BOLT + NUT + PIPE

Lifting heavy objects doesn't require massive strength; the right machinery can redirect force with much less strain. A floor jack doesn't involve much more than a simple machine—in this case, a screw—to redirect your efforts. Heavier objects require a bigger, tougher assembly to resist stripping the threads of the screw under pressure, but with just a few simple parts you can make a jack of your own that does the job.

YOU'LL NEED

- Long steel bolt
- Nut
- Washer
- PVC or metal pipe
- Wrench

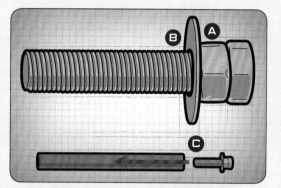

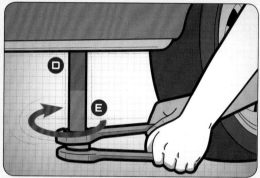

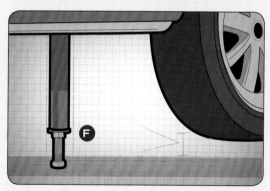

STEP 1 Get a steel bolt that can fit vertically into the gap under the object you want to raise. A bigger bolt (and other parts) will lift more and bear more weight.

STEP 2 Add a nut, spin it all the way down to the base of the bolt (A), and put a washer on top of it (B) to create a stable working platform for the rest of your floor jack assembly.

STEP 3 Put a short length of pipe as wide as the nut and thick-walled as possible on top of the washer (C). Put the assembly under the object to lift (D).

STEP 4 Brace the bolt upright and stable, and then turn the nut (E). As it rotates, the nut will incrementally raise the washer and pipe, lifting the object braced on top of it (F).

031 METAL DETECTOR

BROOM + CELL PHONE + MAGNET

Metal detectors were first created in the late 1800s for mineral prospecting and early medical use (such as finding bullets lodged in human patients)—and later for minesweeping once we started putting things into the ground that went boom under soldiers' feet. This version uses the same kind of Hall effect sensor found in cell phones and other modern electronics, which lets you know you're near metal by picking up changes in a magnetic field. It won't win prizes for beauty, but if you're trying to find a sizeable piece of metal, whether it's a land mine or all the metallic foil and ink in a million-dollar secret stash, it just might do the trick.

YOU'LL NEED

- Hall effect sensor
- Small magnet
- Small speaker
- Battery
- Broomstick

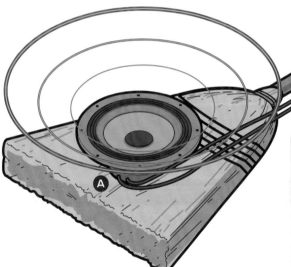

Hall Effect sensor

Small magnet

Battery

STEP 1 Mount the Hall effect sensor at the end of your broomstick; add a small magnet next to it.

STEP 2 Attach a speaker to the other end of your broomstick (A), and add a battery as a power source, several inches down the broomstick from the magnet (B).

STEP 3 Connect the ground lead on the Hall effect sensor to the negative terminal on your battery.

STEP 4 Connect the negative terminal of your battery to the speaker, and connect the speaker's other terminal in turn to the "out" lead on the Hall effect sensor (C).

STEP 5 Connect the positive battery terminal to the input terminal of the Hall effect sensor.

STEP 6 Slowly sweep the end of the broomstick with the sensor and magnet around the area you want to search. If you approach a metallic object, the field around the magnet will change shape invisibly, and the Hall effect sensor will pick up the change, altering the output of the speaker. Good hunting!

032 CAN OPENER

CAN + FRICTION

On the move and want to open a can of delicious beans, but have no can opener? Even if you can't reach any tools, all you truly need is a solid, rough surface like a concrete floor, metal beam, or even a relatively flat rock in the wilderness. Just plunk the can down on the surface, and begin rubbing it back and forth. Little by little, the friction will grind away the metal around the lip of the can; after a few minutes, you'll be rewarded with a lid you can easily pry away. Just watch for sharp edges—and remember your Swiss Army knife next time!

033 TRAVEL STOVE

CANS + FIRE

People on the move, from those down on their luck to hardcore survivalists, may travel light, but they still have to eat—and that means cooking. Here are a couple of ways to prepare a meal on the move, whether you're traveling a post-apocalyptic wasteland, camping with buddies in the backcountry, or heating dinner while hitching a ride with a hitman on a cargo train.

PINCH PENNIES (A) A penny stove is made from the ends of two aluminum cans cut off and slipped together, with the top half pierced by several holes around its edge. The central opening, as the name suggests, is covered by a penny once the stove is fueled up with alcohol. Light it up by setting it in a small pool of burning alcohol on a tin can lid; the fuel inside is vaporized by the heat, igniting a ring of gas jets that quickly heat a pot of water (or a can of beans).

BUILD A ROCKET (B) Built to run on solid fuel instead, the rocket stove is made from just a coffee can with a hole cut in its side, and three soup cans within, minus their tops and bottoms: One stacked on another as the "chimney," a hole cut through the second to match the coffee can, for a "hearth" made from a third soup can. Insulated with kitty litter, sand, or gravel, and fueled by small sticks

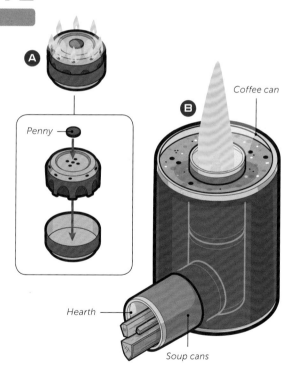

Coffee can

Penny

Hearth

Soup cans

and twigs, the rocket stove channels its flames into a column that'll boil water and cook food easily. (Give this stove a test-run for a few minutes outdoors the first time, to burn off any potentially toxic coatings on the cans' surfaces.)

⊘ ESSENTIAL KNOTS

SQUARE KNOT
One of the basic knots learned by all Scouts, the square knot is often used to secure a rope around an object. It can tie two ropes together, but a sheet bend (see Essential Knots, Chapter 3) is better for the task, as a square knot can come loose if jostled.

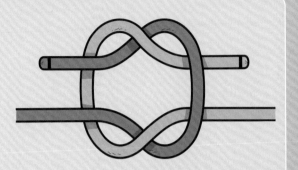

SHOELACE KNOT
The classic tie-your-shoelaces knot, made of a square knot tied with two slipknots.
USED FOR Boot laces, bow ties, and rope handcuffs with a built-in lead.

SURGEON'S KNOT
Multiple twists on bottom (and sometimes top), lays flat when tied with cloth.
USED FOR Holding sutures and bandages.

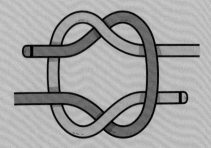

THIEF KNOT
Ends of the knot are on opposite sides instead of parallel.
USED FOR Quick tamper-evident container. (Anyone re-tying the knot is more likely to make it a regular square knot.)

HALF-HITCH

The simplest form of knot, a half-hitch is just a length of rope encircling an object, and crossed over itself. It's insecure on its own, but is the basis for some very secure ties.

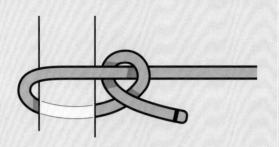

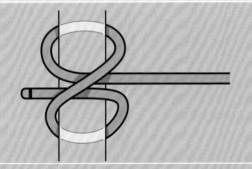

CLOVE HITCH

Easily adjusted by pulling either end of the rope to expand its diameter.

USED FOR Starting or finishing lashing solid objects together, such as wooden poles.

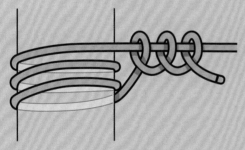

ROUND TURN AND TWO HALF-HITCHES

A fast, simple tie. More turns and hitches can be added for extra secutiy.

USED FOR Tying rope around a fixed object to anchor something, like a boat to a tree, or hitching a horse to a fencepost.

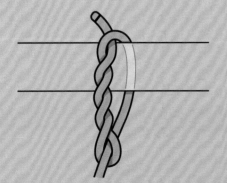

TIMBER HITCH

A half-hitch, followed by turns of the rope around itself. Another half-hitch makes it a Killick hitch.

USED FOR Securing chains or rope around logs, branches, and poles; towing or dragging long, heavy items.

034 IR CAMERA
CELL PHONE + IR LED

In 1800, Frederick Wilhelm Herschel discovered that a thermometer's temperature changes near the light from a prism, proving invisible infrared energy could still be sensed and refracted just the same as visible light. Most modern electronic cameras use a bank of little sensors which pick up both visible light (380–700 nanometers), and IR (700nm–1mm). That extra input isn't usually necessary for your average selfie-taker—but with a little modification, you can use a camera to see in the dark. Got a cell phone to spare?

TEST YOUR PHONE Aim a remote control at the cell phone's camera. If the flashing LED is visible on screen, it's capable of picking up infrared light. (Some cameras have an IR filter between the lens and the imaging sensor, but dismantling the phone to remove it risks damaging the sensor.)

LIGHT THINGS UP Add an infraed LED and battery to the back of the phone for a small, close-range source of IR illumination; more LEDs (and batteries) will weigh more, but will also shed even more "light." As long as you don't approach any security cameras capable of seeing IR (see item 098), you'll be the only one with eyes in the dark.

035 FISHING TACKLE
SAK + PAPERCLIP + FISHING LINE

Stuck in the great outdoors without a fishing pole? Or maybe you need to reel in something that's not a fish, but still important? Remember what I keep telling you about paperclips? With just a few parts, you can put together a makeshift fishing "pole," and be ready to go fishing, whether you're looking for dinner in the woods or just hooking and reeling in something up to your height.

This is a pretty simple contraption: Just tie one end of your fishing line to one of the tools on your Swiss Army knife, and then tie the other end to a paperclip with one end bent open to act as a hook. This setup might not win you any beauty prizes, and its fish-catching qualities are dubious (especially without bait), but it can still work. Just cast into water, or lower the paperclip-hook end to whatever's below you, and then reel it in by winding the line around the handle of the knife.

For heavier objects that can't be snagged by the paperclip hook, use the SAK itself as a hook. Tie the line to the keychain eyelet, partly unfold a tool such as the can opener, and then lower away!

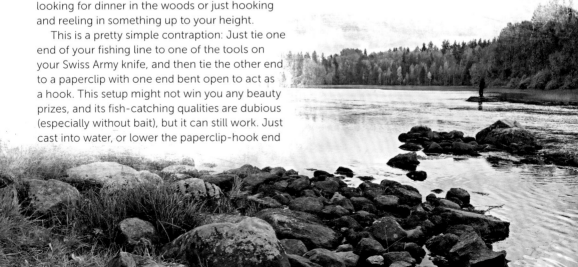

036 COMPASS

PIN + MAGNET

Compasses work by being magnetized so that they orient themselves toward the magnetic poles on Earth. As a side effect, they're also sensitive to other more localized magnetic fields, which means a compass is great for searching out hidden mag-locked doors, for example. If you don't happen to have one, here's how to make do.

YOU'LL NEED

- Small piece of metal
- Magnet
- Cork
- Bowl

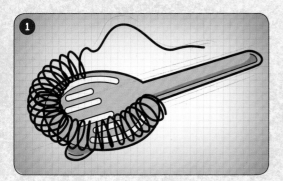

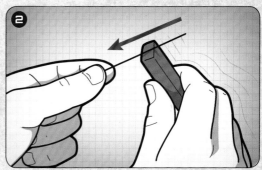

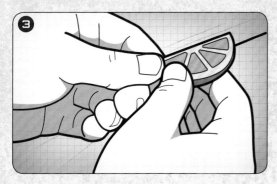

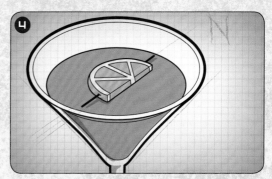

STEP 1 Find a small piece of metal—a safety pin, paperclip, or even part of a mixologist's stainless-steel strainer—to act as your compass needle.

STEP 2 Rub the end of the needle against the magnet about fifty times, drawing it over and over in the same direction as if sharpening a knife; the metal will be magnetized from the repeated contact.

STEP 3 Insert the compass needle through a cork, bit of lemon peel, or something else that will float.

STEP 4 Place your needle and float in a bowl full of water (if you only have a martini in a cocktail glass, that works too). Hold it steadily or set it on a level surface, and the needle eventually will align with north and south. Close to a strong nearby magnetic field, the compass needle will turn to face it instead.

037 ARC LAMP

CARBON ROD + BATTERY

One of the brightest sources of light comes from electrical arcs—the same you find in welding (see item 127) and lightning strikes. In fact, this same principle is what led to the invention of lightbulbs, but sometimes you need something a little brighter than what you'll get from a regular fixture or flashlight. Luckily, a few modern parts can create a brilliant pre-modern electric light.

ACQUIRE CARBON RODS The heart of an old arc-lamp is carbon—the same stuff that makes up graphite in pencil 'lead,' and certain welding rods. If you don't have either of those, cut open the square plastic casing of a non-alkaline battery, remove a cylindrical cell, cut open the top, and pull the central carbon rod out (A). Repeat to get at one more. (You can also find them in non-alkaline batteries such as C- or D-cells.)

PREPARE YOUR ELECTRODES Scrape the surfaces of the rods clean, then sharpen their tips to create a more focused point for electricity to conduct through. Get two lengths of copper wire, and wrap the end of each wire around the bottom of each rod (B).

MAKE SOME LIGHT Attach the ends of the wires to the positive and negative terminals of a large power source such as a lantern battery or 18-volt power-tool battery (C). Without touching them bare-handed, bring the two sharpened carbon rods close together and electricity will arc between them (D). Move them apart slightly, and the electrical current should continue to flow, creating a brilliant light (E). This puts out a lot of UV light, so it'll hurt your eyes if you're looking at it without eye protection (see item 128).

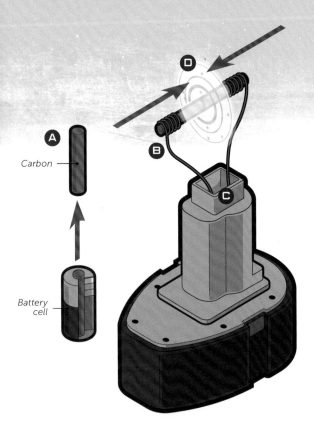

Carbon

Battery cell

038 FIRE STARTER
BATTERY + WIRE

You're cold, you're tired, and the weather is getting worse and worse while you wander the outdoors. Building a fire would help warm you up—but how can you start one without a lighter or matches? Here's how.

YOU'LL NEED

- Kindling + accelerant
- Piece of metal
- Battery (e.g. 9-volt or from a cell phone)
- Gloves (optional)

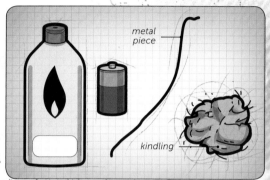

metal piece

kindling

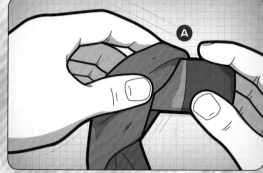

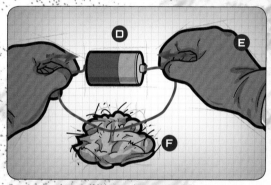

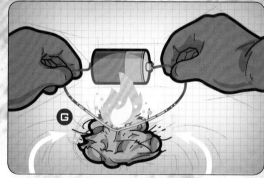

STEP 1 Gather your kindling. Add any accelerant you can find: lighter fluid, oil, even sap flowing freely from a tree's bark.

STEP 2 Find a small flexible piece of metal, like the steel tweezers in a Swiss army knife, or the nickel-chromium wire found inside a toaster or hair dryer.

STEP 3 Clean off the terminals on your battery (A) in order to get a good area of contact with the metal strip your prepared in Step 2.

STEP 4 Stay very close to your kindling and shield it and your battery from the elements. Touch both ends of your wire or foil to the battery terminals—you might want to have gloves because this can get hot—and touch the midpoint of your wire to the lightest kindling (E). The electrical current should heat up the wire until it can create a spark in the kindling (F).

STEP 5 Gently blow on the spark and carefully add more tinder until you have a flame (G), then add more fuel to create a full-fledged fire.

THE SCIENCE BEHIND
STUN GUNS

You've probably heard that distinctive crackling sound, sometimes followed by another sound: the thud of someone falling to the ground, dazed or unconscious. Yep, someone's just been tased. Electroshock weapons, more commonly known as tasers or stun guns, are used to incapacitate targets with electrical pulses that temporarily overwhelm a target's nerves and muscles.

Two things make up electrical power: voltage, the difference in electric charge between two points; and current, or how quickly that charge flows. High current and low voltage can get you a lot of heat and light, which is how electric-arc welders (see item 127) and incandescent lightbulbs (see item 037) work. Meanwhile, high voltage and low current get you a lot of power, but only a little at once. Think of touching a doorknob after walking across a carpet in your socks—that tiny spark can be as much as 50,000 volts, but the low current means you just get a painful zap.

Stun guns deliver high voltage in bursts; each one lasts only microseconds, but a stream of them overloads your nerves and forces muscles to work hard but inefficiently. A brief shock causes muscle spasms and serious pain; several seconds means complete disorientation and paralysis. Electroshock weapons are "less-than-lethal," but they can cause breathing difficulty since your diaphragm is a muscle, and in some rare cases they can stun your heart muscle too—which can ironically be solved with another shock (from a defibrillator) to reset your pulse.

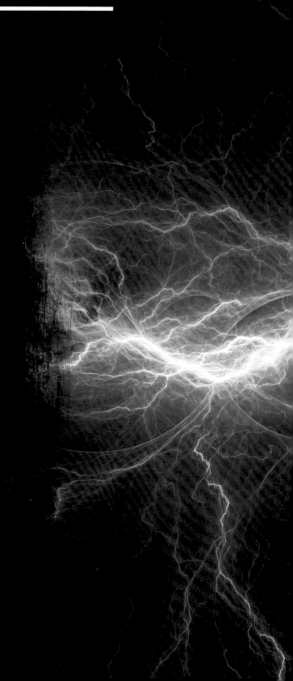

039 LEYDEN JAR

JAR + ALUMINUM FOIL

Back in 1745, Ewald von Kleist zapped himself on a nail stuck through a cork on a medicine bottle after touching it to a static generator made of a ball of sulfur; Pieter van Busschenbroek, from Leyden, Holland, repeated the experiment in 1746, and after that scientists started carrying around jars full of stored electricity to use in science experiments. Unfortunately for von Kleist, all the publicity went to van Busshchenbroek, and the name "Leyden jar" stuck. But no matter the name, the principle is the same: This is a capacitor for storing electricity, charging and discharging it more quickly than a battery. Here's how to test one out for yourself—no thunderstorm needed—and make your own primitive battery (or really primitive stun gun).

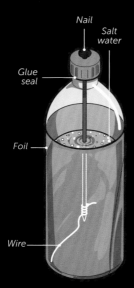

Nail

Salt water

Glue seal

Foil

Wire

STEP 1 Wrap some foil around a cylindrical plastic container such as a small bucket, a water bottle, or even an old film canister, keeping the top of the jar uncovered. Fill the jar about three-quarters with water, and stir in just enough salt to make the water cloudy. Alternatively, you can line the inside of the jar with foil.

STEP 2 Drive a nail or screw through the top of the bottle, long enough to dip into the salt water solution inside (if you use a foil lining, connect the screw to the inside foil with wire). Add glue or cement around where the shaft, lid, and container meet, to keep it thoroughly sealed.

STEP 3 Charge the jar by with an electrostatic current—you can do this by rubbing a plastic rod or pipe with a bit of fur or wool. After a set number of strokes, touch the rod to the nail on top of your jar, and you may see or hear a tiny spark as the charge moves from one object to the other. Each cycle charges the jar further.

STEP 4 Discharge the jar by touching the outside foil lining and the nail at the same time, and you'll get a noticeable zap from the buildup of static electricity. Bigger jars hold more power, so treat them like any other electrical source. Keep your jar away from high-static environments such as ionizing air purifiers, or active electrical storms; the charge that builds up passively can be dangerous, even deadly.

040 BURNING LASER

FLASHLIGHT + LASER

Ever since the first laser was invented back in 1960, people have found endless ideas for this technology—including eavesdropping (see facing page)—but among the most famous is the idea of a laser weapon, like the lightsabers in *Star Wars*. We're not quite there yet, but we can definitely use lasers for cutting and other tasks. This might not burn a hole through a roof all that easily, but in some places it's still considered a weapon, and for good reason. Wear eye protection rated for the laser type if you have it, don't aim the laser at a reflective or light-colored surface, and never at vehicles or living things, especially not someone's eyes—a laser like this can instantly cause injury, even blindness.

YOU'LL NEED

- Mini Maglite or similar flashlight
- Class III-B laser diode from a DVD-writing drive (a CD-writing laser won't work)
- LM-317 chip
- 3.3-ohm resistor

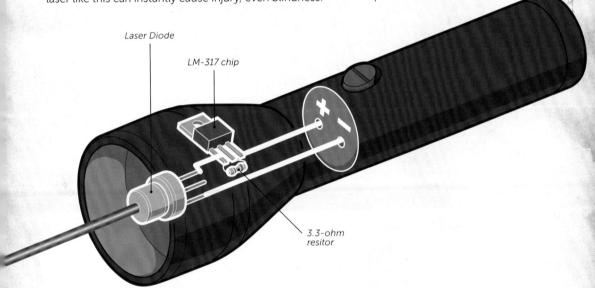

Laser Diode

LM-317 chip

3.3-ohm resitor

STEP 1 Take the casing off of an old DVD burning drive, remove the laser assembly, and disconnect the entire laser diode. There are a lot of small screws and connections to remove, and the diode itself is fragile. If the diode's housing (and lens) is damaged or lost, various electronics companies sell replacements.

STEP 2 Remove the front cover, lens, and reflector from your flashlight, then take out the bulb.

STEP 3 Connect the negative and positive leads in the flashlight that had led to the bulb to the matching terminals on the diode (the third terminal is unused).

STEP 4 This laser won't function very long without a driver in the circuit. To make it last longer, solder the ends of a 3.3-ohm resistor to the output and adjust terminals of an LM-317 chip, then connect the adjust terminal to the positive lead on the diode, and the input terminal to the flashlight's positive lead.

STEP 5 Take aim at a target such as a match head or a balloon, and turn on your laser beam. It works extremely well on darker-colored substances; you can light a match, pop an inflated balloon, or even burn a hole in dark paper or electrical tape if the beam is steady enough.

041 LASER MICROPHONE

Eavesdropping on a conversation doesn't necessarily mean having to bug a phone or go old-school by putting your ear to a keyhole. It doesn't even have to actually involve sound . . . well, kinda. Here's how you can use light—specifically, lasers—in order to hear sound.

YOU'LL NEED

- Solar panel or photocell (from a solar lamp or automatic night light)
- Laser diode, like the kind found in a high-grade laser pointer or CD player

STEP 1 Connect your photocell to an audio source. You can solder the two leads of the photocell to the wiring from a pair of headphones, one pin to the red and white wires, the other to the black wire, and then plug the jack into the input on a laptop or other playback device.

STEP 2 Mount your laser on a steady surface, and aim its beam at the target you want to listen in on. A normal laser is good, and an infrared laser is even better if you can find one: the beam won't be visible, and will work great even through clear window

glass, which is of course mostly transparent to light—including lasers.

STEP 3 Position the photocell in the laser beam's path where it reflects off your target; the steadier both laser and photocell are mounted, the less interference you'll have.

STEP 4 Now, pump up the volume! Sound waves that vibrate the object will cause the reflected laser beam to fluctuate minutely, and your photocell will pick up those vibrations, turning them into sound.

042 PHOTOPHONE

LASER + TRANSFORMER

Invented in 1880 by Alexander Graham Bell, the photophone was the precursor to the telephone, turning sound into light and back. Bell's photophone used light focused from mirrors, which vibrated to conduct a speaker's voice from a microphone. A modern version and transmits information using a modulated laser beam instead, receiving the transmission with a photocell the same as a laser mic (see item 041). Here's how to build your own 'phone.

YOU'LL NEED

- Audio transformer (from a speaker)
- Microphone or other audio source
- Laser pointer
- Photocell
- Stereo or PC speaker

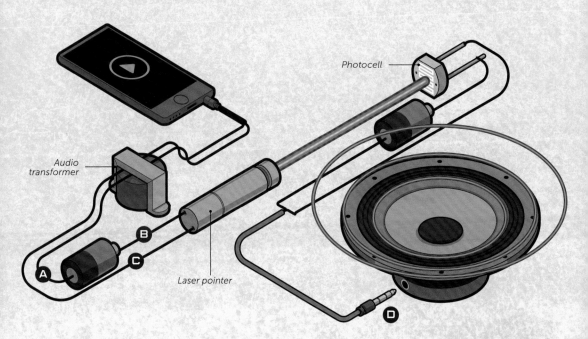

Photocell

Audio transformer

B

C

A

Laser pointer

D

STEP 1 Connect the leads from an audio cable to the leads on one side of an audio transformer, and plug the cable into an audio source, such as a music player, or a laptop with a microphone.

STEP 2 Open up your laser pointer and remove the battery, then wire one of the leads from the other side of the audio transformer to the battery's negative terminal (A).

STEP 3 Connect a wire from the positive end of the battery to the terminal inside the laser pointer (B), and

another wire from the laser pointer's casing to the transformer's remaining free lead (C).

STEP 4 Connect the terminals from your photocell to the inputs on a speaker, and turn on the speaker (D).

STEP 5 Start the playback device, speak into the mic, then aim the laser at the photocell (a laser can "transmit" from a fair distance). The electrical impulses from the playback, passed through the transformer, alter the laser's output, which is turned back into sound by your receiving-end speaker.

043 SPEAKER

CUP + MAGNET + WIRE

All sound comes from vibration, starting with the object in question, transmitted through molecules in the air bouncing off each other, and arriving at your eardrum. Speakers operate by creating sound waves through vibration, generated by an electrical current acting on a magnet. If you find yourself in need of a sound source, you don't have to hit up an appliance store so long as you've got a few of the right pieces.

YOU'LL NEED

- Coated copper wire (usually covered in something like a green enamel)
- Small rare-earth magnet (for example, the type found in a computer hard drive)
- Plastic party cup
- 2.5mm audio jack

STEP 1 Wind the copper wire as many times as you possibly can around the base of your plastic cup; as with anything that creates an electromagnetic field, more windings means a stronger field. Ensure you're using coated wire, so that it doesn't act like just one single winding.

STEP 2 Scrape bare the ends of the coated wire to expose the copper underneath, expose the positive and negative leads inside the wire leading from the audio jack, then attach them to each other.

STEP 3 Tape or glue your magnet to the bottom of the plastic cup.

STEP 4 Plug the audio jack into your phone or other audio source, and turn on the music. Electrical current should run through the wiring, creating an electromagnetic field that causes the magnet to vibrate in sync with it—and thus oscillating the cup just like the cone of a speaker.

COULD I DO THAT?!

The basic principle behind a microphone is that sound waves are picked up by a diaphragm and conducted through a magnet, which is connected to the electronics that turn the sound into a signal. Meanwhile, on the other end, those electrical signals are used to make a magnet cause a diaphragm to vibrate, giving off sound waves.

In short, a microphone and a speaker do basically the same thing—so you can adapt one into the other, but since it's literally being used the "wrong" way, you'll have to do some electrical work, and you'll get only limited use from either.

MacGyver used a pair of palm-sized speakers from a stereo to rig up a broken pay phone missing its handset. Luckily, the major parts that make up a microphone are already found in a speaker, so that part is taken care of. Hooking one up to transmit sound means having to wire it to the leads that a microphone would use, either through wiring in a telephone, a full-sized professional XLR cable (the ones with three pins leading to three holes in a socket), or other connectors such as the audio jack on your headphones.

Could you do this yourself? A definite yes! Depending on the wiring and plug type you're working with, you'll just have to figure out how to link it up. Since a speaker is intended to project sound, it will have a limited auditory range (bass speakers won't conduct the high tones in your voice very well, for example) and it might need a pre-amplifier connected to boost its pickup. In fact, the parts inside larger speakers are too big for your voice to easily move the diaphragm at all. On the other hand, in some cases, if you have just a set of earphones, you can plug it right into the port where a microphone would go. (This also means that you can plug a microphone into an output, if you have the right kind, and create a tiny speaker!)

044 BUGGED STEREO

CELL PHONE + SPEAKER

You don't need to rig your living room with ultra-sophisticated, high-tech, miniaturized bugs to listen in on folks, or dismantle a pay phone. All you need is hi-fi—or even lo-fi—audio, and a mobile phone you're willing to put to unconventional use.

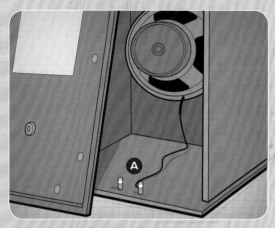

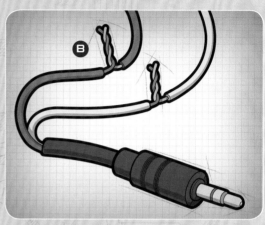

STEP 1 Open up the speaker housing on your audio setup, and locate the positive and negative wires on a tweeter or similar small-sized speaker (A).

STEP 2 Swap the positive and negative leads on the speaker, and then attach a 2.5-millimeter audio jack to the speaker wires (B).

STEP 3 Turn on your cell phone, set it to silent, and adjust the settings so that it automatically answers any call when a headset is plugged in.

STEP 4 Plug the audio jack from Step 2 into the phone, and then hide the phone inside the speaker housing (remember to charge it in between 'missions' or plug it into a charger with its cable also fed out of the back of the speaker) (C).

STEP 5 Call the rigged-up phone and, if you did everything right, it should automatically answer (D). With the speaker's leads swapped, and plugged into the phone, it will perform like a limited microphone for picking up any sound or voices in the room.

DIY SPY DRONE

CELL PHONE + PLASTIC BAG

Unmanned balloons have been around since at least the 3rd century in China, when paper "sky-lanterns" were used for military signaling, though it wasn't until 1783 that a couple of French guys built one big enough to fly untethered. Then again, neither had bad guys cornering them with guns as far as we know. But if you need an eye in the sky and don't have a helium tank or a spy plane, you can use the same basic technology—so long as you don't mind risking a cellphone in the process.

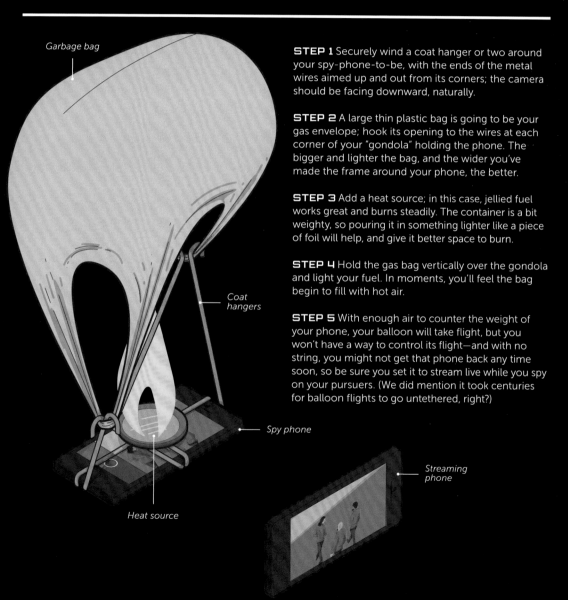

Garbage bag

Coat hangers

Spy phone

Heat source

Streaming phone

STEP 1 Securely wind a coat hanger or two around your spy-phone-to-be, with the ends of the metal wires aimed up and out from its corners; the camera should be facing downward, naturally.

STEP 2 A large thin plastic bag is going to be your gas envelope; hook its opening to the wires at each corner of your "gondola" holding the phone. The bigger and lighter the bag, and the wider you've made the frame around your phone, the better.

STEP 3 Add a heat source; in this case, jellied fuel works great and burns steadily. The container is a bit weighty, so pouring it in something lighter like a piece of foil will help, and give it better space to burn.

STEP 4 Hold the gas bag vertically over the gondola and light your fuel. In moments, you'll feel the bag begin to fill with hot air.

STEP 5 With enough air to counter the weight of your phone, your balloon will take flight, but you won't have a way to control its flight—and with no string, you might not get that phone back any time soon, so be sure you set it to stream live while you spy on your pursuers. (We did mention it took centuries for balloon flights to go untethered, right?)

046 HYDRAULIC SYSTEM

SYRINGES + TUBING + SKELETON

The science of hydraulics has been around since irrigation techniques and water pumps were invented thousands of years ago in Ancient Egypt and Greece. In modern times, that science is applied in heavy machinery, such as the hydraulic cylinders that control the linkage on an excavator arm. You can apply that same science at home—maybe not quite with the same immense power, but it's great for adding moving detail to a Halloween scare.

YOU'LL NEED

- Medical rubber tubing or aquarium air line
- Plastic syringes
- Halloween skeleton

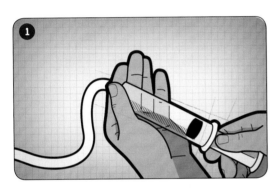
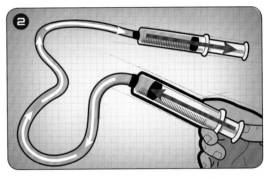
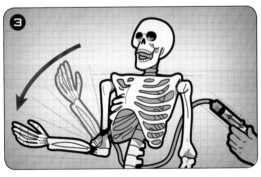

STEP 1 Attach a length of tubing to the tip of a syringe, and draw back the plunger to fill its cylinder and the tubing with water. For added effect, you can add food coloring or other dye to the water.

STEP 2 Attach another syringe to the opposite end of the tubing, and test this setup by pressing the plunger. Water can't be compressed like air, so pressure will force the other syringe plunger to back up as water flows between them.

STEP 3 Pick a spot on your prop that you want to make move; for example, the arm on a lightweight

Halloween skeleton. Attach one syringe to the upper arm with tape or zip tie, facing its plunger end toward the forearm, then while the arm is flexed, tie the plunger's end close to the crook of the elbow. When you press the plunger on one end of your hydraulic mechanism, the plunger at the other end will extend the forearm as it moves.

STEP 4 Repeat steps 1 through 3 as needed on your prop wherever you want to make it move. It helps to keep all the control syringes in a bundle together, and if you make your tubing long enough, you can even operate your prop from a short distance away!

047 PROSTHETIC MAKEUP

TAPIOCA + GELATIN + COCONUT OIL

You can craft some convincing cosmetics and disguises using this faux-latex method.

STEP 1 Mix 1 cup (240 mL) cold water with ¼ cup (60 mL) tapioca flour and 1 tablespoon (45 g) coconut oil. To create soft skin, use one packet of gelatin. For firmer tissues, use 1 ½ packets; use two for tougher cartilage-like props for ears or noses. Add liquid makeup or food coloring for skin color.

STEP 2 Heat for about five minutes until the mix dissolves and thickens, stirring continuously. Cook for about a minute longer, then let it cool for about 10–15 minutes.

STEP 3 Once it's cool enough to handle, pour the mixture into a mold or pastry bag, or onto a solid surface, to shape it. Your creation will retain its shape once it sets, and can be attached to your skin with cosmetic glue or with more of the mixture dissolved in water. Your props and prosthetics will move and feel like the real thing, and should last a couple of days.

YOU'LL NEED

- Water
- Tapioca flour
- Plain gelatin
- Solid coconut oil
- Food coloring or liquid foundation makeup

048 FAKE BLOOD

FOOD COLORING + CORN SYRUP

Fake blood needs the right color and consistency for realism. On the fly, mix thick liquids (like chocolate syrup) with red ink, cranberry juice, and the like. If you have time to prepare, here's a better process.

MIX IT UP Combine dark corn syrup in a 3-to-1 ratio with red food coloring, then add a drop or so of blue or green to give it an appropriate dark-red shade.

MAKE A SPLASH With a little water, you can thin your blood substitute out to spray or splash around.

ADD GORE Thoroughly whisk in a bit of cocoa powder to give an extra realistic opaque look. Sprinkle in some dried onion bits to soak in the mix and take on a "clotted" texture.

049 STAGED MURDER SCENE
PROSTHETIC MAKEUP + FAKE BLOOD

So, you want to stage a location where someone was taken out by a hit man? With any luck, these tips can help you create a believable scenario, whether it's for making a movie just like one of Bozer's, or faking someone's demise to throw real hit men off the trail. It might not fool CSI techs, but you're going for drama, not DNA evidence.

Start by imagining how the "kill" played out, and as you imagine how the scene went, change the room to suit—scatter papers, knock over furniture, maybe even break a window or mirror.

The finishing touch is photographic proof of the kill. Use a flash only to add as much illumination as is needed; less is more, and means the viewer fills in the gaps with their imagination. The "victim" should lie entirely slack, staring blankly off-kilter, eyes heavy-lidded—"dull surprise" is a good way to emote if you're pretending to be a dead body.

050 ACID NEUTRALIZER

CANDY BAR + ACID

Sulfuric acid is nasty stuff. It won't dissolve flesh the way you see in movies, but it does cause some serious chemical burns, and if your eyes or respiratory system are exposed to it in vapor form, you're in for a world of hurt as it'll cause nerve damage and blindness and irritate your respiratory system, leading to impaired breathing or worse. So you might just want to carry some candy bars with you, because they can literally be what stands between you and a caustic fate.

To put one to use, just slap that tasty treat over the crack on your leaking barrel or vat of acid. You might go hungry, but you won't dissolve.

No, I'm not joking: sulfuric acid (H_2SO_4) has an exothermic reaction to sugar ($C_{12}(H_2O)_{11}$), giving off heat and producing steam (good ol' H_2O), sulfur dioxide (SO_2) vapor, and a lot of carbon (plain ol' C). Combined with the rest of the candy bar's ingredients, you get a dense, tarry material that's perfect for sealing that caustic leak. Your dentist might tell you to avoid sweets, but in a situation such as this, I'm pretty sure you'll be forgiven if you choose to pack a few on your next mission just in case.

051 LITMUS TEST

CABBAGE + PAPER

Unsure what that substance is, but don't want to risk your safety by touching (let alone tasting) the stuff? You can start by testing its pH levels with nothing more than a cabbage and a bit of kitchen time.

STEP 1 Finely chop up half a red cabbage (sorry, the green variety won't work), and boil it in a pot with 3 cups (720 mL) of water.

STEP 2 Let it steep for 10 minutes or so; once it cools, strain out the solid material and you're left with a pot of purple liquid.

STEP 3 Drip some of the liquid into a container along with a sample of what you want to test—even solid substances mixed with water can be tested. You can also soak strips of blotting paper in the liquid, let them dry, and use them as test strips. The anthocyanins in the cabbage that give the vegetable its red-purple color will change when exposed to your test substance: Acidic materials will turn the cabbage juice pink to red, while neutral-pH substances like water will turn the test strips bluish, and exposure to alkaline substances will result in a green to yellow color.

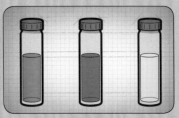

052 SYRINGE

PEN + EYEDROPPER

A syringe or pipette is essential science and medical equipment, whether you're a tech in a science lab, an unfortunate heroin-using convict, or tending to the injured in battle or an emergency room. If you need your own in a pinch, you don't have to be an addict or a medic; just determined and patient.

YOU'LL NEED

- Ballpoint pen (preferable clear plastic)
- Paperclip
- Heat source
- Hydodermic needle or air-pump needle (optional)
- Eyedropper squeeze bottle
- Floss

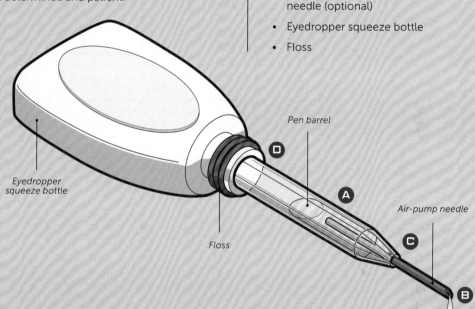

Eyedropper squeeze bottle

Pen barrel

Floss

Air-pump needle

STEP 1 Take apart the ballpoint pen and cut the barrel down to the last couple of inches (5 cm) (A).

STEP 2 Insert a paperclip into the opening at the tip of the pen barrel, and use a flame to gently heat the plastic so that it constricts around the metal shaft of the paperclip. Once the whole thing cools, carefully pull the paperclip straight out.

STEP 3 Pull the nib off of the pen's ink reservoir, and file it to a point for a quick-and-dirty injection tip. Alternatively, if you have a spare air-pump needle (B), you can clip off its end and cut the tip to a 15- to 25-degree angle, and file the tip to a sharp point, or simply break a fresh hypodermic needle off of its plastic housing if you have one to spare.

STEP 4 Replace the sharpened nib, or insert the air pump needle or hypodermic into the hole at the end of the pen barrel (C).

STEP 5 Empty an eyedropper squeeze bottle and remove the tip, then insert the back end of the pen barrel into the bottle's opening (D).

STEP 6 Tightly tie a length of floss around where the pen's barrel inserts into the eyedropper bottle, or superglue the two together.

STEP 7 We don't advise using this on a living subject unless absolutely necessary, but whether used as a syringe or pipette, you can draw up and dispense fluids by squeezing the eyedropper portion.

053 PRINT DUSTING

TAPE + POWDER

The science of forensics and criminology has included dusting for fingerprints since the early 20th century. It's made it that much easier to catch criminals red-handed (or bare-handed), since each fingerprint is unique to the finger of the person it is found on. Here are the basics of what you need to know in order to start dusting for prints yourself.

FIND A LATENT PRINT At a crime scene, anything and everything could have been handled by the perpetrator, so take the time to examine all surfaces closely—eventually you might see a faint impression left behind by the natural oil secreted from skin, usually on smooth, metallic, or glassy surfaces.

ADD DUSTING POWDER The next step is making the latent mark more visible—to do that, you'll need something that sticks to the fingerprint. On a light-colored surface, you need to gently sprinkle on a pinch of a dark powder such as charcoal dust; darker-colored surfaces

can have any prints brought up with a light-colored dust such as baby powder.

BRUSH AWAY The challenging part comes in properly removing the excess powder and only leaving behind that which clings to the oils in the latent print. You can get some of the dust away with a gentle puff of air, but a broad, fine-bristle brush (like the kind used for applying makeup) is even better, as you can use it to gently apply the dust to the print, and then carefully whisk away any extra—but use a very fine hand and be very patient, in order to avoid distorting or entirely wiping away the print.

TAPE IT UP To keep the print stable, you need to transfer it to another surface: A wide strip of clear tape is the perfect substance. Pull a sizeable strip off of a roll of tape, and smoothly apply it to the dusted surface, with the print in the middle of your tape. Press the tape down, and then steadily pull it away again, and fold the tape's sticky side against itself to seal the print inside the plastic layer.

054 STATIC PRINT LIFTER

BATTERY + MYLAR

When a person touches an object, the oils secreted by their skin leave behind a copy of their fingerprints; similarly, they'll either pick up or leave behind dust—which is everywhere, since it's made of microscopic particles of pretty much anything. You can't lift shoe prints the same way that you would dust the area for fingerprints, but dust is easily drawn by static; the ability to generate an electrostatic charge, combined with a ground connection and a medium to capture the dust, can give you an image of someone's footwear. Here's how you can try lifting a set of shoe prints yourself with a DIY contraption.

YOU'LL NEED

- Metallic plastic film such as a mylar balloon, or window film tint

- Metal for a ground connection, such as a steel plate, flattened can, or sheet of aluminum foil

- Electrical source such as a 9-volt battery, stun gun, disposable camera flash capacitor, or Leyden jar (see item 039)

- Small foam paint roller, brush, or sponge

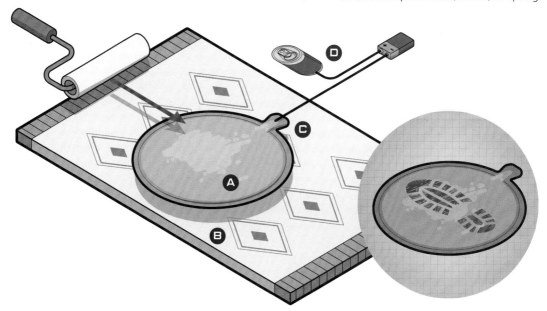

STEP 1 Lay your film sheet over the area you want to try lifting a print from (A), and set your ground plate (B) a short distance away.

STEP 2 Connect one terminal of your static source to the ground plate (C) and the other terminal to the film (D). If you're trying this with a stun gun or other large object, you can connect its terminals to the plate and film with wiring.

STEP 3 Activate your electrical source: Connect the battery or Leyden jar to the terminals, activate

the stun gun for a couple of seconds, or discharge the flash capacitor by winding up the camera and pushing the shutter button.

STEP 4 Allow a few seconds afterward for excess static charge to dissipate, then lightly run the roller over the film to help adhere dust underneath to the film's surface.

STEP 5 Disconnect your electrical source from the film, and carefully lift it off the floor to avoid smearing or blurring the captured print.

MOVIE PROJECTOR

BOX + LENS + DRILL

If you find yourself lacking a projector and want to watch an old family film—or maybe your favorite movie on a big screen instead of peering at the one in your hand—you can turn a simple cardboard box into your own full-size media display. (Popcorn not included.)

YOU'LL NEED

- Shoe box
- Magnifying glass (or adjustable projection lens)
- Cardboard or foam board
- Glue or tape
- Smartphone
- 8-millimeter movie film (optional)
- Power drill (optional)
- Flashlight (optional)
- Pencils and wire hangers (optional)

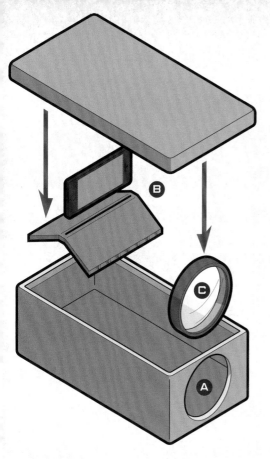

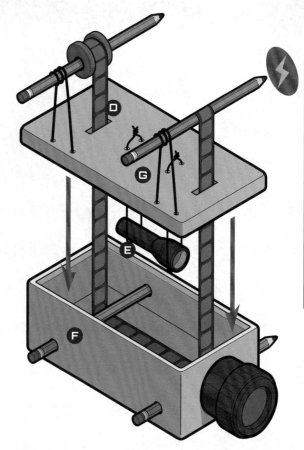

STEP 1 Draw a circle on one end of the box, using the magnifying glass lens as a guide, and then cut the cardboard out (A), and glue or tape the lens into place in the opening.

STEP 2 Measure and cut a piece of cardboard or foam board the width of the shoe-box interior, and twice its height. Make another cut halfway through the cardboard, and fold each side of the cut in opposite directions (B), to use as the base for your phone's stand.

STEP 3 Tape your phone to the stand, and place it inside the box, then turn on its screen. Slide the phone on its stand backward or forward to adjust the focus, while aiming it at a wall or sheet to serve as your viewing surface.

STEP 4 To use this setup as a projector for older movies on film, replace the magnifying glass with a projection lens (C), cut an opening near the front and back of the shoe-box top (D) to serve as entry and exit points for the film, and bend a pair of lengths of

wire from a coat hanger to hang a small flashlight in the middle of the box, close to the lens and at the same height in the middle of the box (E).

STEP 5 Pierce through the box at the same point as the two cuts in the lid in Step 4, below the height of the lens and flashlight. Place a pair of pencils, wooden dowels, screwdrivers, or other rods through these holes to feed the film through the box (F).

STEP 6 Twist another pair of wire lengths each in a tight loop in their middle around a pencil, and attach them upright on top of the box, over the cuts made in Step 4 (G). Set the film's feed spool and take-up spool on these stands, and run the film from the feed spool through the openings and under the rods.

STEP 7 Start the movie on your smartphone, and turn up the volume or connect to a speaker nearby. With an old film strip, turn on the flashlight inside the box, and turn the take-up spool by hand or with a power drill clamped onto the pencil you're using as an axis. It's showtime!

CHAPTER 3

TRAPS
+GETAWAYS

CATCH THE WAVE

Understanding the nature of light isn't only useful in physics class—it might just help you rig a trap or stage a getaway. As with many of MacGyver's best tricks, the key is to combine several different types of science into just one hack. You can't just focus on mechanical things and expect to be successful every time.

WHAT IS A WAVE? In order to understand light, you need understand the nature of waves. A wave is a disturbance that moves. One great and well-known example is a wave in the ocean, which was likely the first thing that came to your mind. Let's look at what's known as a periodic ocean wave to illustrate four key characteristics: amplitude, wavelength, frequency, and speed.

The amplitude is the size of the disturbance—in the ocean, this would be the height of the wave. The wavelength is the distance from one wave crest to the next crest. If you look at how often a wave crest passes by a certain point, that is the frequency. Finally, the speed—as you might guess!—tells you how fast a wave is moving.

But waves don't just happen in water. You could shake a horizontal string to make a wave—this is essentially what happens when you pluck a guitar string. Sound is also a wave. It's a wave, a moving disturbance in the air caused by the compression of air molecules. And yes, light is also a wave, but light is a little more complicated.

SHEDDING SOME LIGHT Visible light is an electromagnetic wave. This means that it is an oscillation of electric and magnetic fields. Unlike sound and water waves, light doesn't need a medium to travel through. In a way, the medium for magnetic oscillations is the electric field (and the opposite is true for the electric oscillations). This means that light can travel through empty space—as of course occurs When light comes all the way from our Sun to the Earth.

Although it doesn't need a medium, light still has the other characteristics of a wave. Its amplitude is how we describe brightness, and its speed is a universal constant—that much bandied-about concept, the speed of light, which is approximately 186,000 miles per second (300,000 km/s). That's fast enough to go around the Earth in just one-tenth of a second.

The wavelength of light is also important. Humans eyes can only detect only a small range of wavelengths from about 400 to 650 nanometers. We identify the larger wavelengths as the color "red" and the shorter wavelengths as "violet," with the rest of the range making up the colors of the rainbow.

CRANK UP THE RADIO But what about radio waves? Perhaps you need to triangulate to find the location of a radio signal, rather than anything involving visible light. (See The Science of Radio Direction Finding, and item 065, for more.) Well, there's some good news. Radio waves are still electromagnetic waves. They have the same wave speed as visible light, but

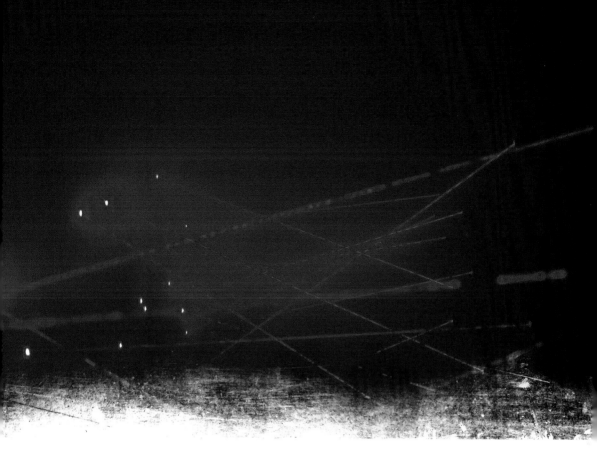

use a different wavelength. Radio waves can have wavelengths over several feet long, instead of the super tiny ones in visible light.

WAVES, WAVES, AND MORE WAVES!

There is a giant range of other electromagnetic wavelengths, which includes microwaves, infrared, ultraviolet, and even x-rays. If you have a firm understanding of electromagnetic waves (or EM waves, as the cool scientists sometimes call them), then you might even be able to trick a surface-to-air missile (see item 078). This is exactly what MacGyver does when he creates some chaff to save his aircraft from imminent destruction.

FUN WITH LASERS A laser is just a special way to make light. The light produced from a laser has some important properties. First, it is monochromatic. This means that it is just one color (and thus one wavelength) of light. You can make this color red, green, violet, or even an infrared wavelength if you like. Second, the laser light is collimated into a tight beam such that the wave of energy travels in the same direction with very little divergence. Lastly, laser light is in phase. The wave crests of the EM wave are all aligned.

Since it makes a narrow beam, the laser light can travel over large distances and still create a visible spot. You can use this laser as a tripwire or even as a remote trigger that will disable multiple bombs at the same time (see items 073 and 075). One thing you might need is a beam splitter, which turns a single laser beam into two. It's really just a piece of glass. When light interacts with a transparent surface, some light is transmitted through and some is reflected; this is how you get split beams. You might already know this and not even realize it: When you look through a window at an angle, it's possible that you can both see through it and see a reflection at the same time!

ROPE

Whenever you're restraining a struggling bad guy, tying objects together, swinging across a chasm, or climbing a cliff, you're gonna need rope. Cordage has been a major part of human civilization from prehistory onward, although the materials used to create it have changed and expanded from natural grasses and hides to include cotton, silk, plastics, metals, and even glass. All of them differ in tensile strength, flexibility, and more, but rope is still pretty much the same thing no matter what: a long, flexible material, braided, woven, or twisted together, and put to endless uses. Listing all of them could fill a book of its own and then some, but here are just a few examples to consider.

TRIP WIRE Traps often need triggers—and for something subtle, fishing line, twine, or even a sturdy vine (see item 087) does the job. To literally trip up an assailant, paracord or heavier line strung taut at ankle height works wonders.

STRUCTURE In the wild, shelter is always a prime concern. Rope can hold up a tarp for a simple tent, or lash branches or logs for a nice sturdy lean-to.

WEAPONS From a simple garrote to a sling (see item 103) to bolas (see item 056) or even whips and nunchaku (see items 093 and 094), cordage can play a part in protecting yourself.

FUSE Setting a villain's stolen cash pile on fire and lighting a pyrotechnic distraction from a distance both require a fuse. A length of cord covered in a fast-burning fuel such as kerosene or smoke powder (see item 101) can be the perfect time-delay setup.

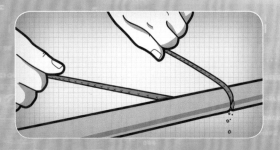

SAW Narrow cordage such as curtain wire, paracord, and dental floss can be used to cut through objects ranging from other ropes to iron bars. Apply an abrasive powder or paste (even toothpaste) to up the friction!

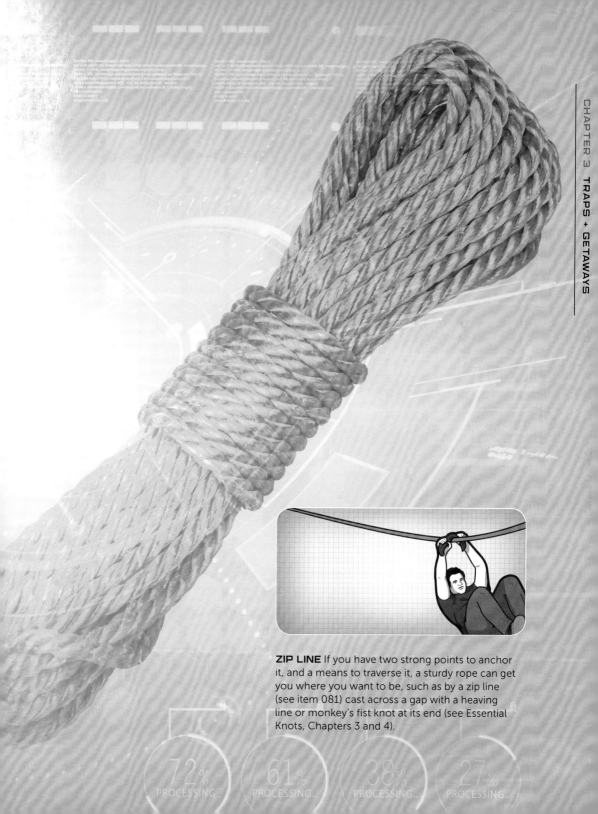

ZIP LINE If you have two strong points to anchor it, and a means to traverse it, a sturdy rope can get you where you want to be, such as by a zip line (see item 081) cast across a gap with a heaving line or monkey's fist knot at its end (see Essential Knots, Chapters 3 and 4).

72% PROCESSING..   61% PROCESSING..   38% PROCESSING..   27% PROCESSING..

056 STRAITJACKET

TARP + BUNGEE CORD

When the bad guy you need to bring in isn't all that compliant, and you're out of zip ties and cuffs, there are still ways to keep them in control. Boas subdue their prey by constriction, while spiders wrap their prey in silk to bind them tight, and unruly mental patients were historically confined to straitjackets. Here's how you and a partner can put that same kind of constricting power to use.

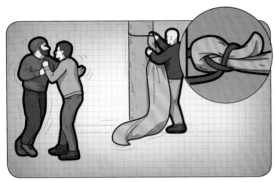
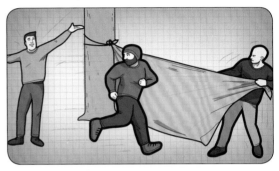

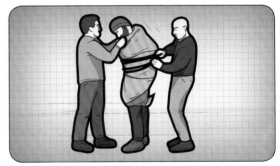

STEP 1 While your partner on the op keeps the subject distracted, quickly unfurl a tarp (or net or sheet). If you have a bungee cord, you can hook it through a grommet or netting; otherwise, a rope tied in a sheet bend (see Essential Knots, Chapter 3) to one end of the material can work. Hook or tie the other end to something sturdy nearby such as a pole or scaffold.

STEP 2 Hold the other end of the tarp up and out, horizontally away from its anchor point, and let your partner direct their struggling subject your way.

STEP 3 Once your would-be escapee runs into your tarpaulin trap, quickly wrap it the rest of the way around their body, rolling "up" toward the anchor point. Depending on your target's size, you should have almost two layers (or more!) wrapped around them.

STEP 4 Release the tied end of your rope or bungee cord from the pole, and bind it around your subject inside the tarp, adding a belt or other cord if you need more length. Instead of using just an overhand knot (see Essential Knots, Chapter 1), wind it twice around the tarp, then tie the overhand knot around both turns. The tarp and the altered overhand, sometimes called a "strangler" knot, will combine to trap them and minimize struggle. (Those predatory animals would be proud.) If need be, add any other cord or strap to keep your newly caught target on a short leash.

057 WEIGHTED NET

NET + WRENCH

Ancient Romans seriously enjoyed their gladiator games, and one type of arena fighter was called a *retiarius*—the "net man" who wielded weapons styled after a fisherman's tools: a trident and a weighted net. You and your fleeing felon might not be in the arena, but here's a way to catch him no matter where you might be.

FIND YOUR NET Fishing nets aren't exactly lying around everywhere, but you can still make your own catch net with a heavy cloth sheet, tarp, or camouflage netting, or anything else big enough to envelop your target.

ADD THE WEIGHTS Anything small and dense can weigh down the edges of your net as long as you can attach it; zip ties and small hand tools are a good substitute for the lead weights of a net.

THROW AND CATCH To fully unfurl a weighted net, wind up for the throw, then cast it forward while twisting your arm and wrist; with a little bit of practice and luck, the spinning motion makes the weights spread outward during the throw, trapping a fleeing target under the net. (You can also easily tangle the wheel of said baddie's motorcycle, landing both rider and bike. Use responsibly!)

058 BOLAS

BOTTLES + TWINE

Bolas are primitive hunting tools, historically made of wood, stone, or bone weights tied to the ends of leather or sinew strips. Spun, then thrown, the weights let you launch the bolas far enough to reach your target and the spinning cords tangle their limbs. Found in multiple cultures around the world, some bolas can have as many as nine weights, but the most common have two or three.

BUILD YOUR BOLAS Both the materials and details of the design can all vary, but you really just need two things: small weights, and cordage to tie them together. Some bolas are made by tying cord around the weights, but if your weights have handles, or holes punched through them, so much the better. The simplest design is two weights nearly equal in mass, tied to the ends of about five or six feet of cordage.

THROW FROM THE HIP The low-throw method doesn't involve much windup; just hold the middle of the cord by your middle and index fingers to keep the weights separated below hip-level. Focus on your target, step forward, then swing the bolas back and throw in a low overhand, following through with your arm as you release.

LAUNCH OVERHEAD This method works better for unevenly weighted or three-weighted bolas. Start by holding the cord closer to the lighter end, with your first two fingers once again. It should only take a couple of swings to wind up for a high overhand throw; as with a hip throw, release overhand and follow through. In either case, keep the weights clear of your head and limbs, and it helps to "lead" the target by throwing just ahead of their path.

059 PITFALL TRAP

Old tricks are sometimes the best tricks, and there are few things as time-tested and proven as a disguised hole in the ground. Humans have been using pit traps for millennia to catch animals for hunting or studying, or to stop people by harming or confining them, or both.

MAKE A HOLE If you're seriously looking to drop someone through a trapdoor, the first thing you need is the pit. If you dig it yourself, make sure it's a few feet deep to begin with; it'll at least slow down whoever falls in. The deeper the pit, the harder the escape and the more likely a chance of injury. You'll also have to dig more material out. Of course, if you happen to find a hole or pit already made—such as a hole through the floor of an empty building—then this part is done for you.

COVER IT UP Pit traps being traps, yours must be hidden, or else anyone you're hoping will fall for it will just avoid it instead. Add cover to suit your surroundings: If you're in the wilderness, criss-cross a handful of long thin sticks and branches over the pit, and scatter leaves and other debris atop them. If you're inside an old building, a thin, fragile wooden board hidden under a stained and torn drop cloth takes the place of natural cover.

ADD BAIT Your quarry needs a reason to walk into the trap, so leaving something on or at the far side of the pitfall (such as a valuable two-way radio—see item 065) will hopefully tempt them to walking into the trap. This is a "set-and-forget" arrangement, so make yourself scarce, especially if you mean to slow pursuers down.

060 PERP STORAGE

The Phoenix Foundation doesn't exactly approve of risky methods, but babysitting a bad guy while you wait for a team to take him into custody can waste valuable hours. You can still leave the team a care package, though, made of one apprehended suspect and a few household items.

APPLY BINDINGS Keep your suspect from rabbiting by making sure they can't move. Similar to netting your target (see items 056–057), you need something to ensure their immobility. Roll them up tight in a rug and tie it shut with heavy twine or rope, to keep their limbs by their side and their legs limited in motion.

ENSURE QUIET The last thing you need is your subject escaping custody while you're away, and if they can call for help, then that's one more way for them to get free and disappear once more. Nothing works quite like a simple strip of duct tape plastered over their mouth—just make sure they can still breathe through their nose.

STASH YOUR SUSPECT Once you have the individual in question safely and securely bundled up, a nice wardrobe or closet can make for an ideal villain-storage space. Immobilized, kept quiet, and stashed out of the way while he cools his heels, no one will be the wiser before your retrieval experts arrive.

⬤ ESSENTIAL KNOTS

SHEET BEND

The sheet bend can tie two different sized cords or even two different materials together. Be sure to tie this one with the ends of the two ropes on the same side, or it can easily fall apart under moderate strain.

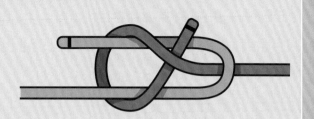

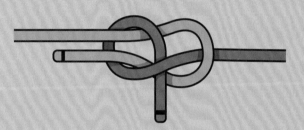

DOUBLE SHEET BEND

Continues the smaller rope's path around and through the sheet bend.

USED FOR Joining very slippery cordage or cloth, like silk cloth and nylon rope.

BINDER TURN

Both ends of ropes point the same way.

USED FOR Hauling heavy objects and ropes, reducing chance of rope ends snagging around or through obstructions.

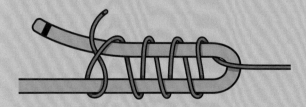

HEAVING LINE

Lighter rope is woven several times through the loop of the other line and finished as a sheet bend.

USED FOR Hauling heavier rope with much lighter line, such as when building a long rope bridge.

BOWLINE

An ancient knot used for centuries, the bowline (pronounced "bowl-in") is one of the four basic nautical ties along with the square knot, figure eight, and clove hitch. Made into a fixed "eye" on a rope, it's easy to tie even with one hand, and easily untied after carrying a load. It's reliable, but can slip if pulled sideways and come loose when not under a load.

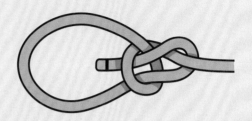

WATER BOWLINE

Adds a clove hitch (see Essential Knots, Chapter 2) before the rest of the knot.

USED FOR Makes a bowline stronger and more slip-resistant in wet conditions.

YOSEMITE BOWLINE

Combines a bowline with a figure eight.

USED FOR Mountain climbing.

KALMYK LOOP

Merges a slipknot with a bowline.

USED FOR Holding down heavy loads that will need quick untying.

061 CAR CATCHER

TIRE IRON + MANHOLE COVER

There's only so much you can do to stop a moving vehicle if you don't have time to set up barricades or spike strips, or can't find a more polite method. But even the road itself can offer a useful, albeit risky, method of keeping a vehicle full of nefarious folks from getting away. A wedge, one of the six "simple machines" of the Renaissance (such as the pulley, screw, or lever; see items 029, 030, and 110, respectively) comes into play: Instead of elevating like a ramp (yet another simple machine) this directs forward motion downward, bringing things to a literal grinding halt.

STEP 1 Get well ahead of your target so you can intercept its path, and find a manhole in the road.

STEP 2 Take the tire iron from the kit in your car, and fit its narrow end into the gap or notch at the edge of the manhole cover. Don't lift the cover; just leave the tire iron very firmly in place and upright.

STEP 3 Keep safely clear as your subject's vehicle approaches, and if they're that determined to keep going, they will take some light damage at the least when they run into the tire iron. The real braking effect comes from the manhole cover being lifted out of its opening and dragging along wedged into their undercarriage. People who've driven over open manholes have had some serious damage done to their vehicles (to say nothing of the impact of a cover itself), and no shortage of injuries. Just like the warning sign says next to those anti-entry spikes, "Severe vehicular damage will result."

062 ENGINE STOPPER

There's nothing better for stalling for time than, well . . . actually stalling something. For example, a getaway car revving its engine as the driver prepares to leave you in the dust. Cars need two things in order to run: Fuel, followed by oxygen for the combustion process. Air comes into an intake, cycles through the engine, then is vented (along with by-products of combustion) through the exhaust. That system must flow openly from end to end in order to work. Block the intakes, and there's no air for combustion. Block the exhaust, back-pressure builds, the engine can't take in new air, and it stalls.

Once you fully block off your would-be runner's tailpipe, whether with a dense wad of paper or the proverbial potato, there's still a chance that a pressure buildup can also blow out something in the exhaust system, even damage the engine in some rare circumstances . . . but you did want to stop the getaway driver from getting away, right?

063 SWISS SEAT

Most climbers, whether construction personnel, window cleaners, or mountaineers tackling cliffs for fun, rely on a harness made of nylon webbing. That said, you might have to do some climbing someday without one—for example, while avoiding gunmen in a high-rise by scaling the inside of an elevator shaft with nothing more than a canvas fire hose. That's where the Swiss seat comes in: a climbing harness made from just a good length of cordage.

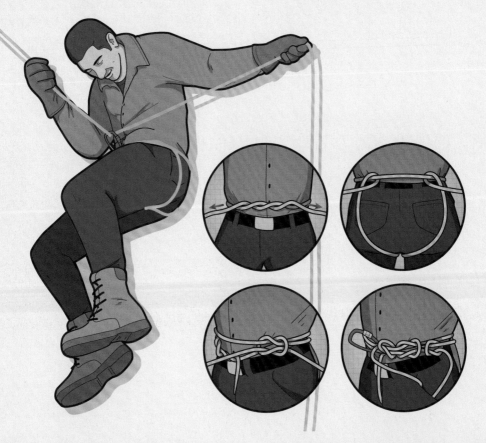

STEP 1 Get 10 feet (3 m) of rope and wrap it around your waist. Make a loop in the midpoint and hold it in your off-hand by your hip. Pull the long part of the rope behind your waist and hold it in both hands.

STEP 2 Tie the rope with two overhand knots in front of your waist, then bring its ends between your legs and around your waist.

STEP 3 Squat down to pull the rope ends outward. Repeat twice more to tighten fully, then tie the ends into a square knot (see Essential Knots, Chapter 2) on the same side of your body you started with in Step 1.

STEP 4 Finish off with a half hitch (see Essential Knots, Chapter 2) tied to the rope's ends close to the square knot for extra safety, then tuck the extra lengths into a pocket, safely out of the way.

STEP 5 Attach a carabiner or, if needed, tie the front end of the harness into whatever rope you're using to descend or ascend.

064 SINGLE-USE ROPE

ROPE + FIRE

A getaway plan will do you no good at all if your pursuers can follow you, especially if, let's say, there's a good number of angry Basque rebels pursuing you through their home territory. They'll be a lot more familiar with any potential escape routes, and won't waste any time trying to cut you off from them.

If you've reached the bottom of your rope after a hard climb to relative safety, a Kamikaze knot tied at the anchor point above (see Essential Knots, Chapter 5) is a potential option, although a highly risky one—and if you spend the time to tie said knot, doing so might just take you long enough for that machine-gun-brandishing mob in the distance to catch up to you.

If you don't need to bring the rope with you once you're on your own two feet safely again, here's another option: Simply light it on fire to both stall your pursuers and secure your safe escape. (After this, if you're still being followed

through the hills and beyond by disagreeable insurgents, there are other ways to keep them off your trail, such as item 070).

Depending on the kind of material that your rope is made of, you might have to add some accelerant, such as oil or kerosene, to speed up the burn. But one quick splash, and once the rope is lit, it'll be like a fuse burning all the way back to the starting point.

Some personnel at the Phoenix Foundation (okay, maybe just Jack Dalton) might have their own opinions on whether or not to let any pursuers start climbing down first before you let the flames climb up to them in return. At the least, it'll leave the bad guys clinging to the cliff side while their buddies rescue them, and maybe give you even more time to get away. But let's be honest: Minimal casualty risks are preferable, and you're supposed to be making a getaway, so there's little reason to wait. Better get moving!

THE SCIENCE BEHIND
RADIO DIRECTION FINDING

Radio transmissions, like all forms of electromagnetic energy, travel in waves. AM radio broadcasts are differentiated by changing the amplitude, or power, of each wave whereas FM is based on frequency—how quickly those waves are generated. Either way, waves are waves, and with the right equipment and know-how, you can catch those waves, and even find out where they're coming from.

Some types of antenna function directionally; that is, by picking up a radio signal more clearly when the physical elements that make up the antenna are pointed toward the signal and less clearly when not aligned. A pair of antennas, set at differing angles from each other (for example, one antenna aligned north-south, and another east-west) and a fair distance apart, will pick up the same transmitted signal very differently.

The signal information picked up by the antenna means you can draw an imaginary line leading from each one in the direction where the signal is strongest. Take two or more of those lines, and follow them away from your antennae toward the transmission. This is called triangulation, since it uses at least three points: two antennas and the signal itself. Where they intersect, you'll have the signal's location and even heading.

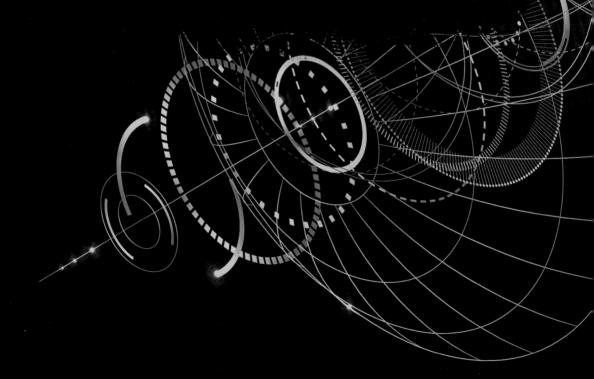

065 SIGNAL RELAY

RADIO + RADIO

Even the good guys get the wool pulled over their eyes now and then. Those unfortunate moments can be opportunities to learn something new or refresh one's memory—and if need be, use the same tricks in kind later on. If you're being tracked by an opponent, hiding or faking a trail leading to you is important—and that includes signals created by any field communications.

It's pretty simple: Turn on a pair of two-way radios, and set one to the channel you want to transmit from. Set the other radio's channel to communicate with whomever you want to talk to, and then bundle the two radios closely together so that they'll relay their transmissions through each other. This works best if you have full-duplex radios so that they can both transmit and receive messages at the same time without issue. If your opponent is able to track the signal of the relaying radio, they'll also find the other radio paired with it, and thus your transmitting frequency is—but you can still lure someone into a trap (see item1 059), or set a breadcrumb trail to stall them while you get some distance (or maybe set up another relay).

066 PERIMETER ALARM

DESK FAN + FISHING LINE + BINDER CLIP

Modern perimeter-security grids use infrared beams, cameras, and more (see item 015), but they're all installed in place. With just a few pieces of fishing and office supplies, you can create an early-warning system that isn't as sophisticated, but is a lot more portable and easier to set up.

YOU'LL NEED

- Sturdy monofilament wire or fishing line
- Binder clips
- Office desk fan

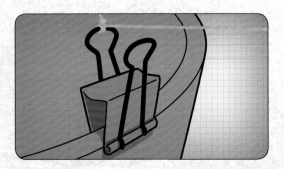

STEP 1 Tie one end of a line to the handle of a heavy-duty binder clip, and then firmly clamp it into place wherever you'd like to monitor traffic. Tied low enough, the line will almost certainly be stepped on rather than tripped over.

STEP 2 Set up a second binder clip nearby (across a step or walkway, for example) at the same height as the first, and run the line through the handle, keeping tension on it as you unreel it back to your hiding spot. If you can angle it around one or two leverage points along the way, like a corner, or the sill of an open window, that's even better.

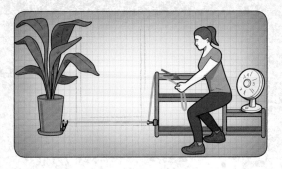

STEP 3 Unhook the positive and negative lead from inside a desk fan's switch, and tie the end of the line around one of the wires. (Alternatively, if it has a stem switch, just tie it securely around that.)

STEP 4 Plug in the fan, and set it somewhere so that when the line is tripped, the tension will flip the switch, or pull the leads into contact and start the fan. Another binder clip makes for a rattling racket, giving you a few seconds to prepare for an unexpected guest's arrival (or a buddy with snacks).

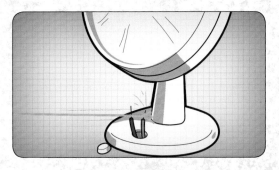

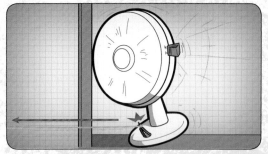

067 PHONE TRIPWIRE

CELL PHONE + STRING

An old mobile phone doesn't often have much appeal compared to a shiny new device. But a less costly or outdated model can still be put to good use even if you can't play the newest games on it. Here's how to turn that kind of cellphone into an intruder alarm.

YOU'LL NEED

- Cell phone with physical keypad
- Soldering iron
- Wire
- Aluminum foil
- Clothespin
- String

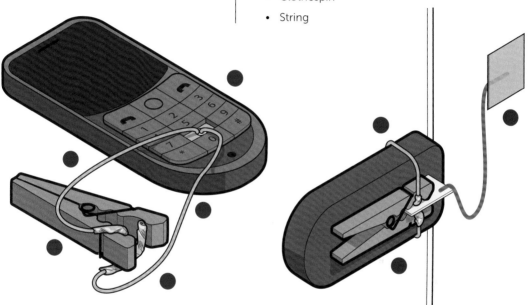

STEP 1 Activate your phone, and set its speed dial function to call you when the 8 key is held down.

STEP 2 Strip the front cover from the phone, and remove the 8 key from the number pad.

STEP 3 Cut off the metal foil under the 8 key (A), and solder a wire to the central point beneath (B). Add another wire to the ring around the center (C).

STEP 4 Run the two wires through the opening cut in the front cover, and reattach the cover.

STEP 5 Strip the far ends of the wires and cover them in a wrapping of aluminum foil (D), then glue or tape them to the inside jaws of a clothespin (E).

STEP 6 Attach the clothespin to the back of the phone (F), and tape your phone securely to a wall next to a door or window you want to set up as your secured entry. (G)

STEP 7 Tape a short length of string to the opposite side of the door or window frame from your phone (H), and tape the end of the string to a small piece of paper.

STEP 8 Insert the paper into the clothespin's jaws between the wire terminals, turn on the modified phone, and your alarm is ready. If someone should open the door or window, the paper will be pulled from between the jaws, closing the circuit, and the phone will speed-dial your number.

068 JOYRIDE-SHARE

PANIC BUTTON + STEALTH + SUV

There are times when you just don't have your own vehicle, and no one on your favorite ride-sharing app will arrive in time (or at all) for you to continue your mission. In such a scenario, why not use your enemy's own resources against them? If you know the minions will come calling when an alarm is tripped, you have a chance to kill two birds with one stone: acquiring transportation while depriving your opponents of the same. It's not exactly a smartphone app, but in an age when you can summon transportation with the push of a button, it's good to keep up with the times.

STEP 1 First and most important part: Press the panic button.

STEP 2 Move quickly (and stealthily!) away from the location and to where you expect your incoming opponent's ride.

STEP 3 Take cover, and wait for assailants to begin looking for you near the panic button site.

STEP 4 With a good distraction courtesy of Step 1, and a bit of luck (since more security-conscious thugs do take their keys with them sometimes), your hands will soon be on the steering wheel of a fully gassed-up armored SUV. Now, drive it like you stole it—because you just did!

069 JET BOOST

JET ENGINE + PICKUP TRUCK

So, you want to go faster? Faster still? A lot faster, so as to escape gun-toting terrorist pursuers, or maybe just really, really show up the muscle car in the next lane? Make like Wile E. Coyote, Darwin Award winners, and speedway show vehicles: use a jet engine! Ever since World War II, jet engines have been boosting heavy aircraft on runways for decades and breaking ground speed records. Here's what to consider, if you want to harness one to outrun hot rods or harmful bad guys.

STRAP IN When I say "buckle up for safety," I mean the engine, too. Jet engines create thrust by compressing indrawn air, combining it with fuel in a high-temperature flow, then blasting it through a nozzle in a superheated jet (hence the name). A fine-mesh screen over the intake will allow air free of debris (since there's a lot less of it at high altitudes). If you don't have time to weld this machine to the chassis, invest in a lot of strong tie-downs and secure anchors—and we mean a lot.

FUEL UP Most jet engines are powered by JP-8 or other liquid fuels, essentially kerosene with protective additives. Diesel is less refined but lubricates like jet fuel, and can substitute at ground altitudes and non-freezing temperatures. Turbines can also use lots of fuel—a gallon or more every minute—but if your emergency getaway takes too long, it's not much of a getaway.

TAKE OFF It takes several seconds for a jet engine to spool up from idle to full thrust, and it'll be loud; earplugs are all but mandatory. Once you get moving, forget precision steering: Thousands of horsepower from a jet means lots of speed in a fairly straight line. This means you'll also need time to cut thrust and put on the brakes later. But, with an open stretch ahead, pursuers will soon disappear in your rear-view mirror.

070 RAFT CATCHER

BARBED WIRE + RAFT

Most means of getting far from a bad guy take place on land; after all, it's where most of us live. An air chase is best left to a trained pilot (if they can't evade an incoming surface-to-air missile, see item 078). On water, unless you're in a speedboat, your two main options will be "paddle faster" or "stop them from paddling after you." The former solution is obvious; for the latter, take a page from cops handling high-speed pursuits on the news, and use an aquatic equivalent of their highway spike strips. A rubber raft is built to take scrapes and bumps from rocks . . . but barbed wire is much more sharp and pointy. Here's how to make it happen. Bring your paddling partner!

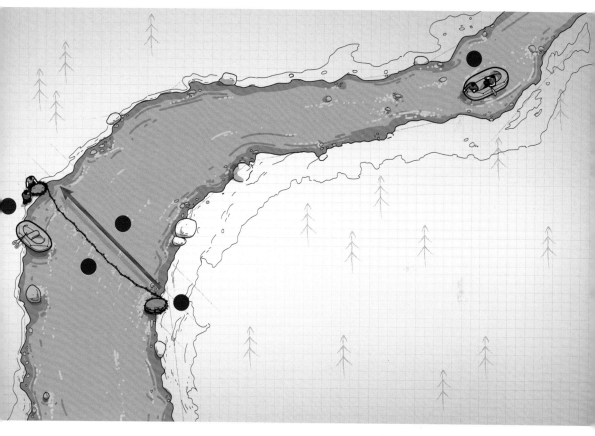

STEP 1 Get a good distance ahead of your waterborne pursuit (A), and anchor one end of a roll of barbed wire on the bank of the river (B) around a heavy rock or the base of a nearby tree trunk.

STEP 2 Paddle upstream diagonally toward the opposite bank (C), unrolling the wire at water level as you go (D) tso as o string the wire perpendicular to the flow of the water.

STEP 3 Anchor the other end of the barbed wire firmly on this side of the river (E); if you're upstream of the anchor point, raise the wire temporarily just enough to get your raft under it and underway.

STEP 4 Once your dinghy-driving pursuers actually reach the wire you've strung, their craft will be hung up on it, and even end up as a less water-worthy vehicle with a lot more holes.

COULD I DO THAT?!

Every airborne balloon, whether full of helium, hydrogen, or hot air, operates on the same principle: A lightweight envelope holding a volume of gas lighter than the surrounding air. Ascent and descent are really the only things the pilot controls; steering is done by finding an air current to ride in a given direction at a given altitude. To make a lighter-than-air craft steerable, it has to have propulsion and a solid frame, thus turning a balloon into a dirigible, such as an old-fashioned airship.

The first passenger-carrying hot-air balloon flight on record took place in 1783 in Paris, with a tethered design launched by the Montgolfier brothers. (Humans may have taken flight much earlier, too: In 1970 and again in 2003, British balloonist Julian Nott used technology created almost 2,000 years ago by the Nazca people of Peru, to build and fly a hot-air balloon, suggesting that they could have been airborne long before the Montgolfier brothers.)

Meanwhile, in one of their missions in the modern day, MacGyver, Dalton, and Riley all found themselves making their escape together on a small backyard trampoline suspended below a cloud of helium-filled balloons, quickly soaring skyward—and bringing themselves down to earth by shooting some of the balloons.

Could you do this? Yes: It isn't exactly easy or safe, but cluster ballooning got its start in 1982, when Larry Walters of San Pedro, California, flew to an altitude of 15,000 feet (4.6 km), borne aloft by helium-filled weather balloons tied to a lawn chair, popping balloons with a pellet rifle to control his descent. In 2017, British thrill-seeker Tom Morgan traveled 1.5 miles (2.4 km) over the South African landscape wearing a harness hanging from his own cloud of balloons. This obviously takes a lot of helium, and it wouldn't hurt to have a hot-air balloonist's training to handle wind conditions and "aircraft" stability—as well as a safe way to get back to ground.

071 CLUSTER BALLOONING

Sometimes, exfiltration from a mission site just doesn't work out. The boat isn't waiting in the surf, the airport is inaccessible, and your getaway car is just plain irreparable—after all, there are limits to what even MacGyver can do. If you have a supply of helium, however, you could find yourself airborne faster than you can say *"Up!"*

GAS UP RIGHT Avoid hydrogen in your high-altitude escape, as it's highly flammable (the Hindenburg disaster wouldn't have been so disastrous otherwise). Propane tanks can give a lift for hot-air balloons, but they're bulky. Helium is inert, with almost the same lifting power as hydrogen; a full balloon can get to about 20 miles (32 km) before reaching atmosphere thin enough to match helium's density.

DO THE MATH Helium lifts 0.03 ounces (1 g) of weight for each 0.26 gallons (1 L) of gas, and larger balloons hold more gas with less "weight tax." For example, your average amusement park balloon holds 3.7 gallons of the gas (14 L) when inflated, and weighs 1/8 ounce (3.5 g), for a net lift of 0.37 ounces (10.5 g). The average human weighing about 137 pounds (61 kg) would need more than 5,700 of those balloons! Weather balloons are a better trade-off: a 5.3-ounce (150-g) balloon, inflated to almost 8 feet (2.5 m) in diameter, has a net lift of at least 15 pounds (7 kg), so you'd start with just nine of them. More balloons equal more lifting power and a faster upward flight.

GET SKILLS (OR LUCK) You could actually get a balloon pilot's license, but why not keep a few basics in mind regardless. First, you only control going up and down. Any other travel happens on air currents, hopefully in your desired direction. Then there's ballast: You have to manage weight and lift distribution, since an unbalanced flight is unsafe, to say the least. Lighter-than-air gas also wants to keep going up. An uncontrolled ascent means overinflated balloons popping, and an unscheduled landing. Keep a means of deflating or simply popping your gas bags—and don't drop or lose it. If all else fails, pack a parachute (see item 072 for more).

There's an old saying: "It's not the fall that kills you; it's the sudden stop at the end." But whether it's a giant umbrella-like round canopy or a smaller wing-like parafoil, a parachute's wind resistance makes the terminal velocity descent a much slower glide. Your average parachute measures between 80 and 500 square feet (7.5–46.5 sq m), but a smaller 'chute could still save you: In 2014, Ernesto Medina of Venezuela performed a 14,000-foot (4.3-km) skydive over Dubai, landing safely with a nylon parafoil measuring just 35 square feet (3.3 sq m). If you have to jump clear of a burning building or an exploding truck carrying a deadly virus, here's how to similarly slow your fall. Grab your trusty Swiss Army knife!

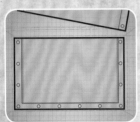

STEP 1 Get a sizeable, sturdy sheet of material, such as a tarp, with enough density to keep air from passing through; this won't work with a crocheted blanket or lightweight sheet. Don't cut too big or your short jump won't give it time to open—let's say 9 by 18 feet (3 x 6 m) at most. Too small, and . . . well, you get the idea.

STEP 2 Cut two even lengths of rope, paracord, or other cordage, about as long as your tarp's short side. Thread the ends into the grommets at the tarp's edges, and then tie them off with a bowline; if you don't have grommets, tie the ends of the cord to each corner using a sheet bend or double sheet bend (see Essential Knots, Chapter 3).

STEP 3 Grab hold of the midpoint of the rope with a hand on either side, and prepare for the moment of truth. Hang on tight to those ropes; you might even want to consider wrapping them around your hands or wrists a couple of times in case your grip slips.

STEP 4 Whether you're a few stories up, or on a moving vehicle, unfurl your canopy by flinging it up and out, and once you feel it catch the air, jump! Tuck and roll as you touch down, and with any luck, you'll find yourself safely on the ground again in one piece, though your landing will almost certainly be bone-rattling.

073 REMOTE WIRE CUTTERS

SWISS ARMY KNIFE + DVD PLAYER + PHOTOCELL

Disarming explosives needs know-how and a physical presence—that of a human bomb tech, or a robot piloted by one. If you'd rather not be up close and personal with high explosives in a dark cramped space, but you're short on robots, try a substitute. Prepare the parts first; this time, your Swiss Army knife is part of the build.

YOU'LL NEED

- DC motor (found in DVD players)
- Servo arm
- 9-volt battery
- Photocell
- Swiss Army Knife
- Laser pointer

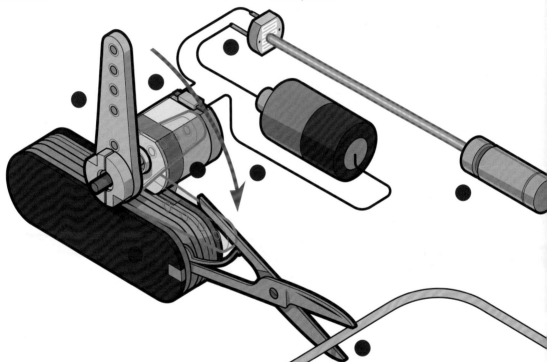

STEP 1 Extract the DC motor from a DVD player (A), and attach a servo arm to the motor's spindle (B).

STEP 2 Connect one terminal of the battery to the motor (C), and the other terminal to the photocell (D), then connect the photocell's other terminal to the motor's remaining terminal (E).

STEP 3 Unfold the scissors on your Swiss army knife (F), then tape the DC motor onto the handle of the knife, with its servo arm positioned above the lever on the scissors (G).

STEP 4 Set your wire-cutting servo in place, with the scissors' blades resting on the wire, and keep the photocell away from light until you're ready to activate it.

STEP 5 Turn on a laser pointer (H), and aim it at the photocell. The light beam will lower the resistance in the photocell and close the circuit, powering the motor and closing the scissors' jaws. If you have multiple bombs to disarm, build and set up more of these devices first . . . and then figure out how to activate them all at once. (See item 075 for more.)

074 TUNNEL BLOCKER

GRENADE + CANDLE

Fragmentation grenades are packed with several ounces of explosives such as TNT or RDX, making these little baseball-sized bombs potent tools of warfare. Normally they're anti-personnel weapons, but they can be turned to a lifesaving task such as a distraction or an escape. And if, for example, you're running through an old smuggling tunnel owned by drug-smuggling criminals who take exception to your presence, you're bound to have hostiles in pursuit.

STEP 1 Plant your grenade. Find a choke point where you can wedge it in place next to a wooden ceiling beam (or even between ceiling and beam) to focus the blast. Sticking it in place will help; if you don't have duct tape or glue, anything tacky could work, like a wad of gum or a generous amount of wax from a candle lighting your way.

STEP 2 Pull the pin. Once it's removed, the only thing holding the safety lever is your hand (or maybe a wet toothpick; see item 076). After the lever is released, you have only seconds to run for cover—such as around a corner in the mine tunnel.

STEP 3 Protect yourself. Even once you're out of direct line of the blast and away from debris, you'll still be dealing with a lot of energy behind you: light, sound, and most important, the intense heat and air pressure from the explosion. Even as you run to get distance and take cover, close your eyes, cover your ears, and open your mouth to account for air pressure changes. (See item 078.)

STEP 4 Wait for the boom. A grenade's blast is lethal at 15 feet (5 m) and injurious out to 50 (15 m); wood can hold up against a great deal of force, but sideways shear forces from a point-blank explosive are a lot to handle. Your confining setup will focus the grenade's brisance (see The Science of Explosions, Chapter 5)—and once the grenade detonates, the path behind you and ahead of your pursuers will be well blocked by fallen debris.

DISARMING MULTIPLE BOMBS

REMOTE WIRE CUTTER + LASER + PRISM

Action movies always focus on cutting just one wire in the nick of time but what if there's more than one bomb, each built by a villainous master craftsman—and all of them are set to go off if any single one of them is disarmed before the rest? Teamwork will only get you so far, especially if there are many bombs; someone might slip or jump the gun. Luckily, light travels the same maximum speed everywhere, so you can enlist it in your Explosive Ordnance Disposal efforts.

MAKE A HALL OF MIRRORS A laser projects a single beam, but a prism can easily split it into multiple beams. Also, light may travel nearly 187,000 miles per second (300,000 km/s), but precision is still important here for timing. Set up every mirror you can find to direct each beam to each bomb, and measure the distance as accurately as you can. Adjust the mirrors' position so that each beam is the same length from the laser pointer to where it reaches each photocell.

READY YOUR EQUIPMENT Prepare a series of remote cutters (see item 073), one for each bomb in your neighborhood minefield, and set them up with the scissors' blades poised on each crucial wire. Keep the photocells covered for now; they'll need light from only your laser. Turn off or cover any light that could activate them and sabotage your own efforts at sabotage (and consider calling the utility company if you need power turned off; see Could I Do That?!, Chapter 4).

ENGAGE THE LASER BEAM Now, with everything in place, and the lights doused, It's time for your moment of truth: Uncover the photocells, and turn on the laser. The beam will be invisible without dust or fog in the air to scatter it, but as each one strikes its target photocell, your cutters will activate simultaneously, clipping their respective wires and sparing you (and your neighborhood) an explosive fate.

076 ROLLBACK CAN

CAN + NUT + RUBBER BAND

Finding your way to safety or rescuing others means having to tread dangerous ground, but you don't need to carry a ten-foot pole to check for traps—just this handheld contraption. When rolled, its movement picks up and stores kinetic energy, which powers its return to you. Along the way, it can test for motion detectors or hidden tripwires, maybe even pick up chemical residue for a litmus test (see item 051). You can even build larger versions to trigger pressure switches and handle rougher terrain, but they all use the same laws of physics and basic materials: a hollow cylinder, a weight, and some stretchy cord.

YOU'LL NEED

- Small paint can or coffee can with removable lid
- Nails
- Rubber bands
- Nut

STEP 1 Pierce the can lid and bottom with two holes equidistant from the middle.

STEP 2 Thread the rubber bands through the hole in the nut.

STEP 3 Put the ends of one rubber band through the holes in the can, and insert one nail through the loops to hold them in place.

STEP 4 Thread the ends of the other rubber band through the holes in the lid. Insert the other nail through the loops to secure them, and then seal the lid on the can.

STEP 5 The nut inside should hang slightly from its weight, not be suspended tautly, and the rubber bands should be a little loose. Roll the can across the ground, and the rubber bands will twist and tighten, absorbing kinetic energy. Once the can stops, the nut will swing it back in the opposite direction, propelled by its own momentum. The rubber bands will unwind, sustaining the momentum and propelling the can back to you.

077 GRENADE PIN

GRENADE + TOOTHPICK

A grenade won't explode the moment you pull the pin—lucky for you if you're still holding the one and can't find the other. But once the spring-loaded safety lever (called a spoon) that was held there is released, it flies off and a fuze is triggered; you have about five seconds to throw your angry little friend, take cover, or both.

No duct tape for the spoon? No paperclip to replace the pin? (Have you even been reading this book?) If you have a toothpick, you might just be able to buy some time with it. Wood has lots of strengths, but it's weak in shear resistance, or how much sideways force it can take (like the lateral force from the spring) before breaking. If the toothpick was in someone's mouth, moisture might swell and soften the fibers; it won't snap as easily, but it'll still eventually bend. Did I mention the fuze only lasts about five seconds?

078 DIY CHAFF

MYLAR + SAK BLADE

Radar tracking works by transmitting a radio signal, and measuring a change in the signal as it reflects off of a moving object, in order to find the target's distance and general size. Stealthy aircraft can deceive radar systems because they're built to absorb radar signals, reduce their apparent size, or otherwise look non-threatening. Conversely, to draw attention on radar—or to distract a radar-tracking surface-to-air missile—chaff is the way to go. Basically a small cluster of chopped wire or metal fibers, aluminum foil shreds, or similar metallic materials, chaff shows up on radar very well, and can even jam it by filling the sky with a cloud of false signals and flooding the radar screen with useless noise.

Are you flying the unfriendly skies in an aircraft without countermeasures? You can still make your own: Pull out your knife, grab a mylar survival blanket, and start cutting it to ribbons. The more shreds that you make, the better, as they'll disperse in the air and create a bigger cloud, and thus more radar interference. Once you've turned your survival blanket into something that'll help ensure a chance to find another survival blanket, dump the heap of chaff into your slipstream, and take evasive action. With any luck, the chaff will draw the missile's attention away from you. If it's a heat-seeking missile, you might have luck with a bundle of flares, but either way, brace for a rough landing afterward just in case!

BLAST PROTECTION

EXPLOSIVE + KNOWLEDGE

An explosion is a powerful expansion of energy (see The Science of Explosions, Chapter 5, and item 074, for more). Being a member of an elite covert organization such as the Phoenix Foundation does involve high-explosive blasts now and then. Whether or not you happen to have your own EOD suit, knowing how to protect yourself from a blast can literally be vital. Here's what to do when dealing with a risk of something going boom nearby.

KNOW THE FORCE A high-explosive blast travels faster than the speed of sound, and can be much more dangerous than just the heat or shrapnel that it sends flying. Close enough, the wave itself can rupture multiple internal organs including kidneys, lungs, and intestines.

SHIELD YOURSELF Obviously, a solid wall or other hard cover is your best protection, especially from debris and heat—just as long as it's sturdy

enough, and far enough from the blast so that your intended shelter doesn't collapse on you.

KEEP AWAY Every blast radiates outward from where the explosive previously existed. Luckily, the inverse square law of physics tells us the farther you get, the more rapidly the energy dissipates. For a given distance, it's at a given strength; twice that is one-quarter as powerful, three times' the same distance is one-ninth as strong, and so on.

ASSUME THE POSITION One final layer of safety is your orientation to the blast. Bombs generally scatter debris in a flower-bouquet pattern up and out; lying face-down with legs together, feet toward the blast, will minimize your profile and shield your organs and head. Close your eyes, cover your ears and open your mouth, then empty your lungs and breath shallowly. It's tempting to hold your breath, but lungs filled with air are the most vulnerable to the shockwave.

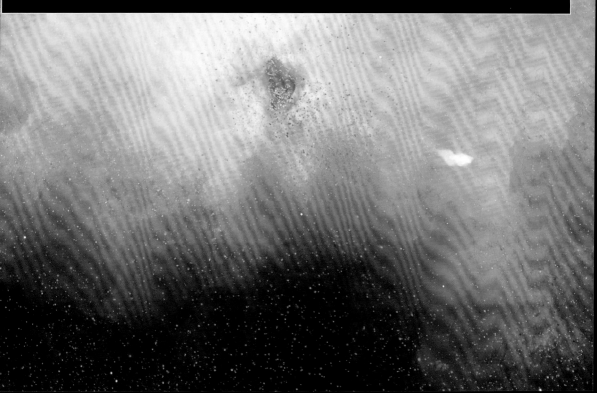

080 AIRBAG LANDING

BODY BAG + FIRE EXTINGUISHER

Making a quick escape sometimes means taking some serious risks—but when your other option is, for example, "stay in a burning building," you're going to be a lot more likely to choose the risky way out. In a high place, an escape is tough without a parachute (see item 071), a zip line (see opposite page), or even a rope to climb. Time to soften your landing instead!

GRAB A (BODY) BAG To start off, you will need something sturdy enough to withstand the impact of a body (namely your own) as well as large enough to take up the same surface area as yourself or larger—such as an air bag, like the ones used to safely break a fall from a height taken in a Hollywood movie stunt.

ADD SOME CUSHIONING You won't just need a wide surface. Just like that air bag employed in a film stunt, your container will need to be inflated. Luckily, with a portable gas-filled container (like an extinguisher full of CO_2 or compressed air and fire-smothering powder), you can have a quick and easy means of inflating your prospective airbag. Just be sure to tape or otherwise secure it tightly against leakage, so that the gas doesn't escape and leave you with a really hard landing. Likewise, don't overfill your airbag. You might think that more gas means more safety, but your airbag is going to need some give so that it will collapse a little on impact, absorbing the kinetic energy of your fall and decelerating your landing enough to make it survivable.

A tightly-filled bag won't be much better than hitting solid ground; you'll either bounce off of it too hard, or more likely, the cushioning will rupture when it takes the blow, leaving you just as bad off as if you didn't fill it with any gas at all.

JUMP FOR YOUR LIFE This is where math and luck intersect, because physics is a harsh teacher. You don't need too much stopping distance as long as you're not jumping out of a high-rise, but your landing is going to be rough. Good luck!

081 ZIP LINE

CABLE + COURAGE

Acrophobia, or fear of heights, is a common thing, and rightly so; climbing up against gravity's pull means storing up potential kinetic energy for a descent—in other words, what goes up must come down. But you can put this to your advantage by turning a sturdy rope or cable into a zipline, whether you're escaping captivity through a mansion's high attic window, or chasing down a frantically fleeing arms dealer on a field mission.

FIND YOUR LINE Zip lines installed in adventure parks are purpose-built, but luck comes into play in finding a good substitute in other places. A heavy steel cable or rope anchored securely with a little bit of sag, free of obstructions, and with a gentle incline is perfect (parks generally max out at 6 feet of drop per 100 feet of travel (1.8m/30 m); a thin length of wire strung loosely between walls and studded with bulbs, not so much.

HOLD TIGHT The next step is ensuring you stay on the line and keep moving, so you need a handhold that'll carry you down its length. A harness such as a Swiss seat (see item 063) hung from a pulley is perfect, but even a short length of rope or sturdy cloth thrown over the line makes for a handhold. Overhand stopper knots (see Essential Knots, Chapter 1) can provide more grip.

TAKE THE LEAP Once you get some forward momentum, your body's inertia, combined with gravity, will propel you down the line. The lower the friction, the faster you'll pick up speed. When you get near the bottom—you did check to see where the line ends first, right?—tuck your legs in for the dismount. If you picked up a generous amount of speed, you need a way of softening the landing. (Hopefully the arms merchant in your sights will help cushion your fall.)

CHAPTER 4
DISTRACTIONS
+DEFENSES

WHERE THERE'S SMOKE . . .

Sometimes you need a little help. You want to do something fun, but the baddies are watching you. That's the perfect time for a distraction: maybe a smoke bomb or a small explosion to draw attention away. Of course, for MacGyver, the solution lies in physics and chemistry coming together.

LET IT BURN Where would we be without the ability to make and control fire? It's no stretch to say that fire is what defines us as humans. It can both destroy and create. It provides light and heat. And it can be both a distraction and a defense.

Any discussion of fire should start with the concept of the "fire triangle." This is an easy way to remember the important aspects of fire. The three sides of the triangle are oxygen, fuel, and an ignition source (usually heat). A fire needs all three of these things to burn. Take away even one of them and you have no more fire. Knowing the fire triangle is not only useful for starting a fire, but also for extinguishing one, since you know what, if removed, will cause the flames to die.

But there's knowing the fire triangle, and then there's MacGyver-level understanding. Let's start from the fundamentals. Fire is a chemical reaction between oxygen and something else (where the something else is most commonly carbon). Remember, there is a difference between atoms (like oxygen and carbon) and molecules (like carbon dioxide and water). Atoms are essentially single particles that you can't easily break apart. Molecules are created by combining multiple atoms through some type of chemical bond.

All chemical reactions involve breaking and forming chemical bonds. If you want to break a chemical bond, you have to add energy—but that means that you can get energy (thermal energy) by forming bonds.

Now we can connect all three parts of the fire triangle to particular chemistry concepts. For

example, let's consider a heat-induced reaction between carbon and oxygen. The heat is the energy you add to the different molecules that the carbon and oxygen are part of—the fuel source and the air, respectively) to break the molecular bonds. After the oxygen and carbon atoms are freed, they combine to form carbon dioxide. And forming carbon dioxide also produces energy . . . even more energy than required to get this chain reaction started. The energy produced is called fire. It doesn't matter if it is a fire from gun powder or a smoke bomb (see items 084 and 103). It's all basically similar chemistry.

THROW UP A SMOKE SCREEN So, it's not that hard to make some smoke. But how do you make enough to sufficiently obscure someone's view of you so that you can make a getaway? There are lots of different types of smoke—but

FIRE
Oxygen
Ignition
Fuel

all of them are made of some type of small particles. It could be unburnt fuel from a fire, it could be some other chemical formed during a reaction, or it could even be tiny water droplets. All of these work the same way.

But if you want to obscure vision, you first need to understand vision. How do humans see things? They use their eyes—simple, right? Well, it's true that humans see with their eyes, but that misses some important points. Seeing is all about light. You need a light (like a flashlight or the sun) to see things. Light from a source travels out in all directions. When light reflects off a surface and then enters your eye, your brain interprets this light to give you a "picture" of that object.

So what does the smoke do? When light interacts with the particles in the smoke, it also gets reflected. The light reflects in all sorts of directions (because of the many tiny particles in the smoke). With the light reflecting off the smoke, much of it can't get to the person or object you want to see. And for the light that does make it to the object, the reflected light then gets scattered again by the smoke. This

leaves no light going into the observer's eye and thus no observations. That's what we call a smoke screen.

MAKE SOME NOISE There's nothing like a nice loud sound to use a distraction or a warning sign. But what is sound? Just like light, sound is a wave (remember how we just learned about waves in the last chapter? Sure you do!). It has an amplitude (how loud) and a frequency (the pitch). But unlike light, which can travel through empty space, sound needs something to travel through. In most cases, this medium is air. A sound wave is a compression in the air. This compression travels through the air from the source to a human's ear.

But how do you make sound? Of course there is always the explosive option, but what about other noises? Any constant tone is produced by some oscillating object. It could be a vibrating plate that pushes the air back and forth. But you can also make sound by moving air in and out of a pipe. This is what happens with an improvised whistle, and something similar is used for an air raid siren (see item 091).

DUCT TAPE

When you think about it, duct tape is pretty miraculous. Jack Dalton would even say it's like the Force: It has a light side, it has a dark side, and it practically holds the entire universe together. It's used for a whole lot more than just patching holes or sticking things together, and while other kinds of tape offer many of the same advantages, nothing else quite takes its place.

GAGS + BONDS An unbound, ungagged bad guy is a mobile, noisy bad guy. If you're short on rope, several windings of duct tape around their ankles or wrists will keep your subject from getting far (if you're the one taped up, see item 019). Duct tape also makes an instant gag (such as in item 060)—a sticky, painful one to remove.

KNOTS Whether you're employing a rough gripping natural rope or slippery artificial fiber, any knot could stand to be reinforced. It'll make untying more tedious, but wrapping a knot and the nearby cordage in duct tape will definitely help stabilize it.

BANDAGES Duct tape can patch up just about anything—including you! To bandage a wound without medical tape or a roll of gauze, duct tape can hold a cloth or gauze-pad dressing in place. Tiny strips cut from the tape can easily work as butterfly dressings.

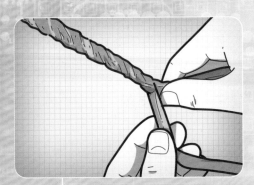

FIRE It smells horrible and gives off a fair amount of smoke (see item 084 for more), but a crumpled ball of duct tape (sticky side out) can be used as a fire starter when there's no other tinder in reach.

CORDAGE It shouldn't be trusted to hold very much weight, but in a pinch you can peel a strip of tape off and twist it tightly, sticky side inward, to create a length of substitute rope, or tear it lengthwise into skinny strips before twisting, to make "string."

CONTAINERS Duct tape sticks very well to a lot of things, including itself, and this can be used to your advantage. Woven or taped together into sheets, it can be fashioned into lightweight containers of practically any shape; use even more tape for handles or shoulder straps.

082 HIGH-PROOF FIRE

ALCOHOL + CIGAR

In the Age of Sail, two of the most important things used and traded by pirates and privateers alike were rum and gunpowder. The strength of alcohol in a barrel of hooch was determined by whether or not a burning ember could ignite a puddle of rum mixed with gunpowder—thus providing tangible 'proof' to the prospective consumer that the alcohol was potent and worth drinking, rather than watered down. That same property can give you a diversion bound to get attention, especially when things really light up.

Any alcoholic beverage that's over 57 percent by volume (that's 114 proof; anything equal or higher in alcohol content is known as "overproof") can be lit on fire, and a bar with its bottles full of high-strength rum, vodka, and more besides, means you have a veritable liquid arsenal at your disposal. Add a burning ember from a local aggressor's cigar to a spill of high-alcohol hooch, and they may end up too busy stopping their favorite watering hole from going up in smoke to stop you from getting away.

083 FLAMETHROWER

PROPANE TANK + INNER TUBE

Flamethrowers have existed since at least the First Century BCE, when Greek soldiers used bellows to spurt a flammable material called naphtha, or "Greek fire," at wartime enemies. Modern military versions have used liquid fuel under pressure, while civilian brush-clearing torches employ pressurized gas instead. No matter how, when, or where they're used, one thing is for sure: Everyone wants to avoid being burned, and you can turn this to your advantage.

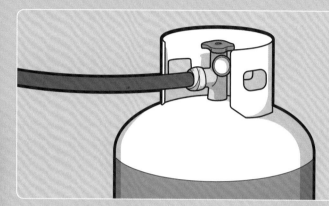

STEP 1 Start with a propane tank (the kind used for barbecues and mobile homes), and attach a hose—flexible rubber tubing is ideal; even an intact bicycle inner tube will work—so long as it's secured tightly. You really don't want this coming loose.

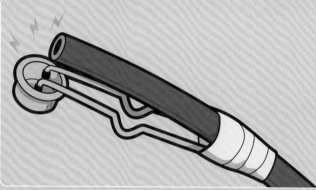

STEP 2 Attach an ignition source to the far end of the tubing. Gas-torch rigs and flamethrowers use either a spark tool or pilot light along with a squeeze-handle or valve, but even a simple road flare will suffice.

STEP 3 Strike your flare alight or scrape some sparks, and open the valve on top of your tank to let the gas escape through the tubing. You won't have long before the propane runs out, and this is obviously really dangerous. But, holding the tank in one hand and the gas-spurting end of the tubing in the other, you'll have a very big billowing jet of flame. (Did I mention this is really dangerous?)

084 SMOKE BOMBS
PING-PONG BALL + STUMP KILLER

The beloved smoke bomb: favored distraction and method of escape for mad scientists, Batman, and ninjas everywhere. But you can't just throw together a couple of chemicals and hope for the best, even in the field, unless you want to risk burns or poisoning (or both). Here are a few quick and handy ways to generate smoke to baffle fire alarms and guards alike.

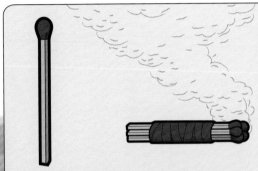

PLAY WITH MATCHES Where there's smoke, there's fire, and in this case, it's literal. Wrap a few wooden matches in a bit of electrical tape, just below the head, and scratch them on a striker to light them up. The initial burst of fire will also set the tape to smoldering, and once you blow out the flame you'll be left with the world's least-pleasant incense stick: plastic-scented! But you'll also have a small, but steady, short-lived source of smoke.

TRY PING PONG They may be hollow, but ping-pong balls are a great way to make smoke. Their brittle but bouncy spherical shape comes from them being made out of celluloid, the same stuff used in old movie film, and this stuff burns pretty well. Chop up a ping-pong ball or two, wrap up the bits in a sheet of foil with a tiny opening for a little bit of air, and set them alight.

STUMP THE ENEMY For a major smoke grenade, combine sugar and potassium nitrate (KNO_3, found in stump remover; also see item 102) in a roughly 2:3 ratio, in a soup or soda can. You can make this mixture even better by slowly heating it in a pan over low heat until the sugar just melts and the two become a goop resembling peanut butter—too hot, though, and your concoction will literally go up in smoke. Add a waxed string or cord as a fuse, and it's ready!

085 ELEPHANT TOOTHPASTE

PEROXIDE + SOAP + YEAST

Exothermic reactions are the type that give off heat as the chemicals combine or break down—and those same reactions often take place very rapidly. The "Elephant Toothpaste" experiment is a great way to safely demonstrate that kind of reaction in front of a science class . . . or, maybe to stop a car full of kidnappers and drug smugglers.

YOU'LL NEED

- 20-volume (6% solution) hydrogen peroxide
- Dish soap
- Food coloring (optional)
- Warm water
- Dry yeast

STEP 1 Pour 1/2 cup (120 mL) of hydrogen peroxide into a plastic bottle or flask; a large container with a narrow opening works best.

STEP 2 Add 1 tablespoon (15 mL) of liquid dish soap to the peroxide; add several drops of food coloring if you want it to be more colorful.

STEP 3 Mix 3 tablespoons (45 mL) of warm water and 1 tablespoon (6 g) of dry yeast in another container for about 30 seconds or until fully dissolved. As the yeast activates in the warm water, it produces an enzyme called catalase, which will react with peroxide (H_2O_2), breaking it down into water (H_2O) and oxygen (O).

STEP 4 Add the yeast mixture to the bottle, and stand back. Within seconds, the reaction will pick up speed—and get pretty hot!—mixing oxygen rapidly with the water and soap, and spraying a jet of foam from the bottle like, well, a giant toothpaste tube. You can scale this mixture up; a gallon jug or two can make enough foam to fill a car interior!

⬤ ESSENTIAL KNOTS

TRUCKER'S HITCH

Highly familiar to truckers, as you might guess by the name, this tie is made from almost any loop in the rope's length, with the end passed around or through a pole or ring, back through the loop, pulled down to tighten the rope, and finished with another hitch or knot. It's great for securing heavy loads (and even as a primitive block-and-tackle pulley—see item 029), but friction can eventually wear through the rope.

SLIPPED OVERHAND LOOP

What we call a trucker's hitch that uses an overhand loop and slipknot.

USED FOR Securing light and medium loads.

SIMPLE FRICTION LOOP

Twists in the bight increase friction on the rope passing through its own loop.

USED FOR Holding heavy loads; the spiral made by the twists compresses the loop at the end.

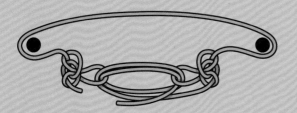

VERSATACKLE

A hitch tied with two overhand loops. Self-locking under tension; mechanical advantage (and wear) increases with each turn between the loops.

USED FOR A rope-based pulley system.

MONKEY'S FIST

A favorite of sailors, historical mountain climbers, and skydivers (as a handle to deploy a parachute), the monkey's fist resembles a clenched paw. Deceptively simple looking, it's made by forming multiple loops, then another series of loops around the first, followed by a third series around the second set but inside the first, sometimes tightened around a central object. Variations are based on the number of loops, the size of material used, and sometimes what's held inside the "fist."

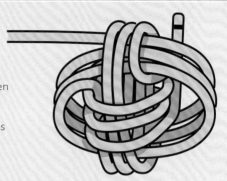

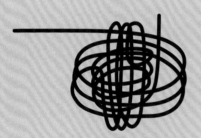

SILK KNOT
Made from small cordage or wire.

USED FOR Big stopper knots on small lines, cuff links.

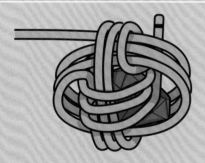

SLUNGSHOT
Made from heavier cord or rope with a weighted object concealed inside.

USED FOR Climbing anchors (jammed into cracks in rock faces); smuggling small, solid objects; considered a weapon in some jurisdictions.

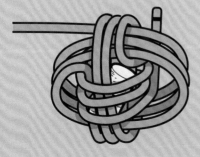

LIFELINE
Tied to the end of a rope similar to a heaving line (see Essential Knots, Chapter 5) without the smaller hauling cord; includes a cork or other buoyant object.

USED FOR Throwing lines between watercraft (with or without nets) or to rescue person overboard.

086 FAKE SNORKEL

REED + ROCK + WOOD

You've probably seen movies or TV shows wherein someone hides underwater, breathing through a hollow bamboo stick or other reed like a snorkel while they swim along to their destination or wait for their pursuers to look elsewhere. I'm not here to tell you it won't work—because it will, as long as you're not too far underwater. (Too deep and you won't displace enough air through your snorkel to take in fresh breaths.) What I can tell you, though, is that if you've seen all those movies and shows, then it's likely that whoever's keeping watch at the site of your mission has also seen them and knows this trick. But you can still make use of it.

Fake them out by grabbing a reasonably sized reed or bamboo shaft in the area—and then look for a chunk of wood and maybe a stone. Wedge one end of the reed into a crack in the wood, and if you need to give it some neutral buoyancy, add the stone and tie in place with paracord, string, vines, or long grass. With a little luck, the wood will bob along under the water's surface, and your fake snorkel will do so above the water, drawing the attention of all those ninja-movie buffs and *Gilligan's Island* fans on your tail. Move quickly, though; this distraction won't hold them for long once they figure out they've been had!

087 TIME DELAY

BAG + ROPE + ROCK

Water clocks and hourglasses were invented a long time before more complex clockwork mechanisms, and both of these devices measured the passing of time based on just the inflow and outflow of a given fluid substance, such as water or sand. The simple principle of mass shifting from one point to another means you can also rig up a primitive counterweight timer, with just a few simple items and somewhere to hang them. Whether this setup is rigged to the trigger of your teammate's spare firearm tied in place and aimed at a container of high explosives, the pin of a grenade, or maybe just a cap gun pointed up into the open air, it's bound to make some noise.

STEP 1 Fill a backpack or other container with sand or water (if your container is waterproof), and tie a length of rope, cord, or vine to the weighted container.

STEP 2 Find a rock or other heavy object to match the weight of the filled container, and wrap the rope around it some distance down the cord's length, so that you have the container at the end, the weight in the middle, and the remaining length of rope free past that.

STEP 3 Hang the rope over a tree branch or hook, midway between the container and the weight, then tie the free end to whatever you want your timer to pull on. The balanced weight of the two objects will keep them in place for now.

STEP 4 Make a hole in your container. Poke a hole in it with a Swiss Army knife, open a nozzle if it's a water bottle hanging upside down, or use whatever other means you can use to get the sand or water flowing out. Once enough mass flows out, the rock will get heavier by comparison, and without the container's countering weight, it'll pull on whatever you've rigged to it—so make tracks unless you want to be there when someone comes to investigate!

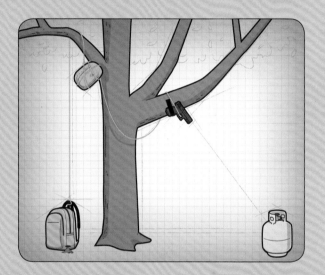

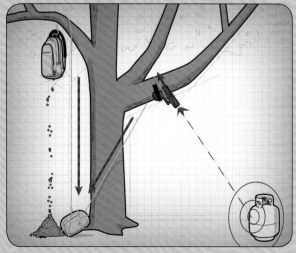

088 GHILLIE SUIT

NET + CAMOUFLAGE

Named after a Scottish Gaelic word for "servant," a ghillie suit is one of the most effective forms of camouflage. Sometimes literally made from the landscape itself, this camo can be foiled by thermal sensors (since the suit holds in heat), but you could be literally standing next to someone wearing a ghillie in the wild and you'd never know. Here's how to make one of your own, whether for stalking notorious criminals through the woods of the Ukraine, or maybe just for paintball or hunting.

YOU'LL NEED

- Fishing net or garden netting
- Loose clothing or poncho in natural or camouflage tones
- Burlap or other rough material
- Cloth dye or spray paint
- Soil, leaves, twigs, and other plant matter

STEP 1 Cut sections of the netting and stitch or glue it to the clothing or poncho underneath, leaving most of the netting hanging loosely.

STEP 2 Cut yourself some strips of burlap—the more ragged, the better. Save some of the strips of cloth as is, and separate the rest into loose threads or use twine or jute thread.

STEP 3 Dye the fabric strips and threads from Step 2 using spray paint or cloth dye in natural shades to match where you'll be hiding—for a ghillie suited to a forest, stick with green and brown shades; to create one for grasslands, use tan and green colors; and so on.

STEP 4 Tie a strip of cloth or a small handful of threads to each junction on the netting. Use a lark's head knot or square knot instead of a simple overhand (see Essential Knots, Chapters 1, 2, and 5) to keep each bundle secure. Add more thread and cloth strips until the whole suit is covered. You can make a quickly-improvised ghillie in the wild with larger branches and other debris tied around dark clothing, but a truly good ghillie takes a while, so be patient!

STEP 5 Finish your suit with small branches, leaves, and grasses tied the same way as the cloth. Put on the suit and roll around on the ground to give it an even rougher look. Good hunting!

089 NATURAL DEFENSES

VINE + WOOD + ROCK

The wilderness is its own tool kit when it comes to creating almost any simple tool or mechanism. You can easily set traps with nothing more than what you find growing or lying around. The possibilities are near endless, but here are a few to start.

VINES Vine plants, such as ivy, liana, grapevine, and more, are found in environments ranging from temperate to tropical, and are naturally self-camouflaging in their home ground. Cut vines to use as sturdy cord for tasks from lashing together sharpened sticks for a palisade, to creating trip wires or a handful of "remote controls" leading off to multiple simple traps, or noisemakers.

WOOD Not just fuel for building campfires, branches and sticks are ideal for lightweight constructions, including arrow shafts, spears, fences, even part of a fake snorkel (see item 086) made from a hollow reed or bamboo shoot bobbing down a stream.

STONES The earth practically grows rocks, and they're not just for throwing as a weapon or distraction, or building fortifications. Tied to the distant end of a long vine, you can rig one or more to fall at a single pull and psych out a pursuer, or as a counterweight for more complex creations (see item 087).

THE SCIENCE BEHIND
TEAR GAS

Tear gas is the layman's term for a riot control agent. The fact is, it's not actually a gas, these agents are either an extremely fine solid powder, or a cloud of liquid in aerosol form, consisting of the main lachrymatory (or "tear-causing") agent and several other substances that burn as fuel for a tear gas grenade, or enhance its effects.

Charcoal (C) and potassium nitrate (KNO_3), both found in gunpowder along with sulfur (S), make up much of the fuel. Potassium chlorate ($KClO_3$) is often found in the mix, and when heated, provides large amounts of oxygen, which helps keep the fire going, and breaks down into potassium chloride (KCl) that adds to the smoke created by the grenade. Other ingredients include sucrose (table sugar, or $C_{12}H_{22}O_{11}$), which melts at a low temperature and helps heat and disperse the lachrymating agent; and magnesium carbonate ($MgCO_3$) which neutralizes any impurities, and also breaks down into carbon dioxide (CO_2) when heated, thus helping to further disperse the gas. Nitrocellulose is yet another ingredient: though explosive when refined, it's made into ping-pong balls when combined with camphor (which is why they're great as smoke bomb fuel—see item 082); lower grade nitrocellulose is used as a binder to hold everything together in a tear-gas ganister.

The main lachrymatory agent in tear gas can be any one of a variety of substances, such as O-Chlorobenzalmalononitrile ($C_{10}H_5ClN_2$) or CS for short. These agents actually have a direct effect on the nerves in the eyes, nose, mouth, and lungs, and are responsible for much of the coughing, tears, and runny nose; dizziness and disorientation also occur, and all these symptoms can last more than an hour after exposure. There's no one antidote for exposure, so the only thing to do is cover your eyes and remove contacts, and wear a high-grade respirator or gas mask; the internet may tell you to soak a rag in ammonia or offer other defenses, but none of them really work that well. After exposure, wash your skin with soap and water (first cold, then warm), and thoroughly wash or discard your clothing; agents can stay active in the fabric for months.

PEPPER SPRAY

HOT PEPPERS + ALCOHOL

Tear gas is made with a variety of lachrymating agents—stuff that make your eyes itch and water and your throat and nose burn. CS is one of the best known, but another is OC, short for Oleoresin Capsicum, or capsaicin. In its pure form, this oily compound tops the Scoville Heat Unit scale at 16 million SHU. Bell peppers have zero capsaicin; the aptly named Dragon's Breath pepper rates up to 2.5 million SHU; refined pepper spray as both a human and wild-animal repellant, meanwhile, can have more than 5 million SHU. You can whip up a quick-and-dirty spray from hot sauce, ground pepper, and water, but to try this formula for making your own, I recommend gloves, goggles, and a mask.

YOU'LL NEED

- Cayenne pepper powder (the fresher, the better)
- Rubbing alcohol
- Baby oil or mineral oil

STEP 1 Mix 2 tablespoons (16 g) of cayenne powder with just enough rubbing alcohol to create a thin paste; capsaicin is an oil, and alcohol will dissolve it out of the powder.

STEP 2 Add 12 drops of baby oil to the mixture, and thoroughly mix everything again.

STEP 3 Strain the solids using a cloth or paper filter such as a coffee filter. This recipe can be scaled up if you want more—4 tablespoons (32 g) cayenne, double the previous amount of alcohol, and 24 drops of baby oil, for example.

STEP 4 Pour the liquid mixture into a spray bottle with a pump. You'll create a short-ranged cloud of mucuous-membrane-burning mist if you unleash this stuff, so just like any other defensive tool, be sure you know what you're using it on.

091 AIR RAID SIREN

PVC PIPE + TRASH CAN + FAN

Civil defense sirens have been in use worldwide for decades and for various reasons; the most well-known use comes from World War II air raid warning sirens, or from tornado warning sirens in the Midwest. Although the sound of this siren is now often broadcast from speakers, it originally came from a mechanism that drew air through an intake, and out through openings in a rotor. Want to generate some incredibly loud and intense tones, whether you're warning of impending dire weather or trying to distract a building full of suspicious security guards? It's time to use the saw blade in your Swiss Army knife!

STEP 1 Get two heavy-duty PVC pipes, one slightly narrower and able to fit inside the other with as little space as possible—the inner, the rotor, has to spin inside the outer, called the stator, in order to make the noise of this siren.

STEP 2 Cut a series of rectangular slots into the rotor and mount it securely on the axis of a spinning motor—a building's HVAC fan, or anything else fixed in place, is ideal.

STEP 3 Cut another set of rectangular slots around the stator; if you want a siren that generates more than one tone, you can cut two sets of slots: a set of four larger rectangles on one end, and a set of five smaller rectangles on the other, for example.

STEP 4 Mount your stator into place around the rotor, fixed in solidly and centered on the axis, so that the rotor can spin inside the stator without rubbing against it.

STEP 5 Add an intake, such as a PVC trash can with its bottom cut out, to focus indrawn air downward along the axis; like the stator in Step 3, make sure it stays secured.

STEP 6 Spin up your motor, and as its RPM increases, the noise from the rotor spinning inside the stator will grow louder and louder. As the rotor accelerates, the air drawn down through the intake into the center of this mechanism will be forced outward through the slots in the rotor and stator, and "chopped" by the moving parts, creating that familiar howling wailing sound!

092 GAS MASK

BOTTLE + INNER TUBE

A gas mask works by filtering your indrawn breath through a canister or other filter attached to the mask, while also protecting your eyes and face from the same substances by shielding them behind a visor. In an emergency, you might not have full-on military-grade protective gear or riot equipment, but you can at least rig up something that will offer you some protection. (The secret is the activated charcoal, but you can even get limited smoke protection with wet newspaper as a filter in the bottom of the bottle.)

YOU'LL NEED

- 2-liter bottle
- Bicycle inner tube
- Aluminum can
- Activated charcoal

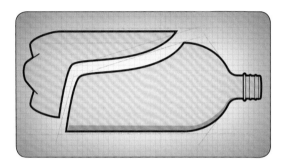

STEP 1 Cut the bottom and side out of a 2-liter plastic soda bottle to fit around your face (A), and edge it with a length of rubber inner tire tubing to create a gasket seal around its edges.

STEP 2 Add another strip of rubber as a headband, and test fit the mask to ensure it stays sealed against your face.

STEP 3 Pierce several holes into the bottom of an aluminum can (B), and fill the inside of the can with activated charcoal granules (C).

STEP 4 Tape the top of the can to the mouth of the bottle at the bottom of the mask, ensuring a tight seal between the two (D).

STEP 5 Pull the mask on, adjust the headband to tighten it around your head and seal the mask's edges against your face (E), then breathe in carefully. As long as you don't inhale too fast or too strongly, any air taken in will pass through the filter, and much of the tear gas or other substances will be absorbed by the charcoal granules in the can.

093 NUNCHAKU

POOL CUE + BAR RAG

A bar fight is always a rowdy affair, and often an everyone-for-themselves kind of event. Pool cues are often a weapon of choice, but you can improve on those and fight your way to safety with just a couple more easily found items.

STEP 1 Start by finding two lengths of wood about a foot long each; a broken broomstick or snapped pool cue from your ongoing bar brawl should be readily available.

STEP 2 Connect your two sticks with a flexible material—another thing bars often have on hand is rags for wiping down tables and bar tops. Secure each end of the cloth to the ends of each stick with zip ties or duct tape.

STEP 3 Like all other improvised weapons in a fight such as this, it might last one swing or one hundred, but either way you now have a pair of nunchaku. Time to become a barroom Bruce Lee!

094 ELECTRIC WHIP

EXTENSION CORD + SAK BLADE

Guards headed your way? Narrow confines? All out of ammunition, and all you've got is a Swiss Army knife and a few sturdy industrial extension cords? A favorite of Jack Dalton (who never fails to mention his junior whip-cracking championship as a kid in Texas), this means of improvised defense might just shock you. Hopefully, though, it'll sting the enemy more than the whip-crack itself!

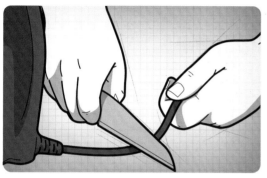
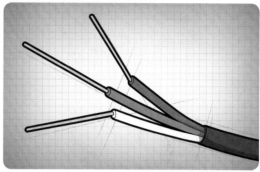
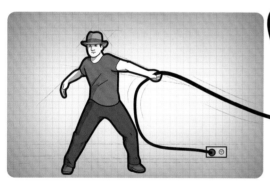

STEP 1 Find the longest electrical cord you can, and cut the head off of the non-socket end.

STEP 2 Strip the main coating from the end of the cord, then strip a couple of inches of sheathing off of the wires, leaving the bare metal wiring exposed. Keep each wire bent safely away from its neighbor (and definitely don't touch the bare ends yourself).

STEP 3 Now for the fun—translation: dangerous—part. You'll have to plug this in to make it really work, because it's time to unleash your inner Jack Dalton (or Indiana Jones, if you're actually Jack). Take aim at your aggressor and crack the whip! Sling it forward under- or overhand, and flick your wrist for bonus points and improved accuracy.

STEP 4 If your aim is true, the real effect comes from the electrical current: There are between 110 and 240 volts of alternating current coming from a socket, depending on where you are in the world, and that means a nasty shock from this whip if its ends touch the target. An aggressor will experience pain and electrical burns at the least, and unconsciousness or worse—but they certainly won't be shooting at you.

COULD I DO THAT?!

BLACK OUT
THE
NEIGHBORHOOD

High-voltage power lines route electricity from a power plant into regions with substations, which then transmit power through lines on utility poles to local neighborhoods, where power is stepped down with utility transformers and distributed to homes and other buildings. Power runs through as many as three cables on each pole, with a fourth acting as a ground line.

In some cases, birds can safely land on a line or a squirrel can run on it without creating a circuit, but when two electrical lines are connected, a short can occur, and power to an entire neighborhood or larger can be knocked out. The outage can last a few seconds before an automatic relay resets, in the case of a temporary short circuit (such as a squirrel zapping itself on two lines and falling off); or indefinitely after a fuse or transformer blows during a longer short-circuit event and needs repairing—such as when a wet or otherwise conductive object is stuck in place, such as a damp towel, or the aforementioned unfortunate squirrel.

Acting on MacGyver's behalf, Bozer once used a wet towel, a broomstick, and a ladder to create a blackout. Staying on a ladder with insulated feet is one way to avoid a ground connection that would let electricity travel through you, and wood is a poor conductor of electricity as long as it is dry; this is why broomsticks are used to deal with electrified objects or people.

Could you do this? Maybe—if you felt like climbing a high ladder up a utility pole, and knew how and where to hit the right lines or damage the transformer—but you should never, ever try it. Local utility lines can carry power at thousands of volts and hundreds of amps; even trained professionals working with the utmost caution have suffered fatal electrocutions while on power lines. Common wisdom is that "volts jolt, amps kill," but enough voltage can still be lethal with minimal amperage. A single residential line has more than enough of both to fry a person as easily as that poor squirrel. (Seriously. Don't do this. We can't stress this enough.)

095 FARADAY SHIELD

TRASH CAN + ALUMINUM FOIL

Back in 1836, Michael Faraday discovered a way to shield a person or object from electricity: An enclosure made of a conductive material such as copper, iron, or aluminum would distribute any electrical field interacting with it without passing through its interior. Large stable fields such as Earth's magnetic field will still pass through the enclosure, and if it's mesh instead of solid, the openings must be smaller than the frequency of the radiation (see below). But to protect sensitive electronics against EMP, you've got a few options.

ALUMINUM FOIL The tinfoil hat–wearing conspiracy theorist crowd are kind of onto the right idea, but just like the garbage can construction, it's best to keep a solid shield around whatever you want to protect. Put your phone or other delicate electronics in a plastic bag or wrap, then add a layer of foil around it; alternate between even more layers for extra secure protection.

MICROWAVE OVEN

Depending on the oven model itself and its age and construction, you may be able to use one as a quick and easy Faraday cage; after all, it's meant to keep microwave radiation from getting out while using that same radiation to heat food inside. Just keep in mind that all microwaves do have some minor non-harmful electromagnetic leakage, based on the size of the holes in the viewing window (and older ones leak more), so this isn't a 100% perfect solution for EMP protection.

GARBAGE CAN
As long as the lid and body of a metal garbage can fit together tightly, you can use one for a Faraday shield. Anything inside has to avoid contact with the metal shielding so as to avoid conduction; you can do that by lining the inside of the entire can and lid with cardboard, and sealing the two together with metal tape.

096 POCKET EMP GENERATOR

Created by a solar flare, nuclear explosion, or other massive power source, an electromagnetic pulse (EMP) is a blast of energy that can affect sensitive electronics, disabling or destroying them. Even if you're no card-carrying villain with a handheld high-tech prototype, you can still build your own EMP device. This one turns the power of a small battery into a high-voltage jolt. Don't use it near any electronics you don't want to risk damaging, and to avoid giving yourself a nasty shock, don't touch any bare wires or the discharging spark gap inside the box.

YOU'LL NEED

- Enamel-coated copper wire
- Plastic box or other small, sturdy, non-metal container
- Glue or tape
- Zip ties
- High-voltage inverter (such as a 6V–12V to 80kV module)
- Small piece of plastic
- Momentary push-button switch
- Rechargeable AA or 18650 battery

STEP 1 Wind the copper wire into a small donut-shaped coil (A) and bind it with zip-ties.

STEP 2 Drill a pair of holes in the side of the box. Insert the ends of the coil into the holes, winding the remaining free wire around the inside of the box (B). Glue or tape the wiring into place.

STEP 3 Connect one end of the wiring to a terminal on one end of the inverter, and glue or tape the inverter into the box. Bring the other end of the wiring close to the other terminal on the same end of the inverter, but leave a one-inch (2.5-cm) gap between the two to create a spark gap. Cover this gap fully with a small piece of plastic to keep the spark from arcing to any other point and shorting the circuit.

STEP 4 Drill a hole in the top of the box to install the momentary switch (C), and connect its terminals to the positive terminals on the battery and inverter.

STEP 5 Connect the battery's and inverter's negative terminal, and seal the box.

STEP 6 Aim the coil at a nearby electronic device and push the button (D). The spark gap creates a quick buildup, discharged into the copper coil to generate a crackling electromagnetic field pulse.

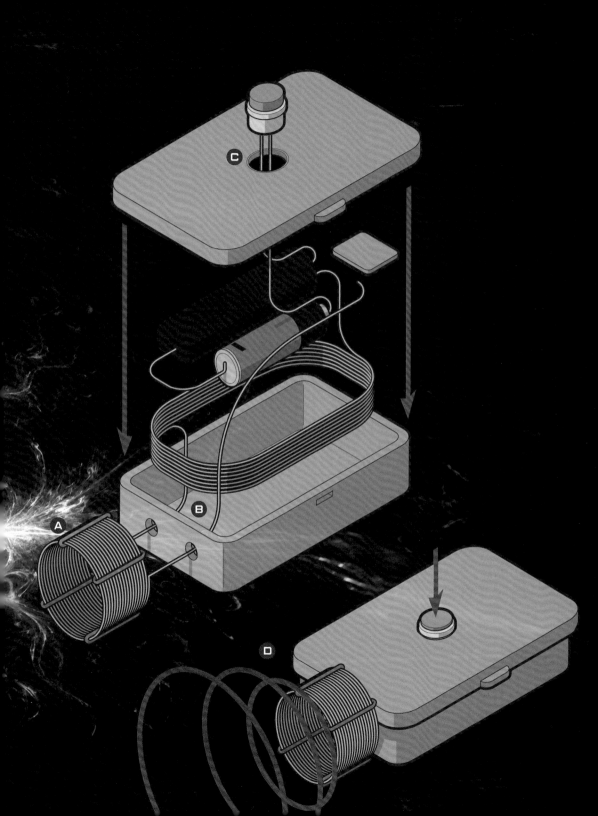

097 EM INTERFERENCE

WIRE + METAL + BATTERY

You've probably heard those weird chirping and buzzing noises coming out of cheap speakers when a cell phone or radio nearby is active, or turned on the radio and heard one channel talking over another. This is interference: A stronger source of electromagnetic energy overwhelming another. It's frustrating or distracting when it happens to you, but the same principles behind this problem can be used to your advantage when you're dealing with someone on an earpiece or handheld radio.

YOU'LL NEED

- Iron rod (such as a heavy-duty nail or pin from a door hinge)
- Coated copper wire
- Battery such as AA or 9-volt

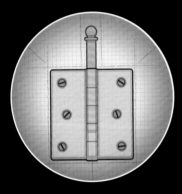

STEP 1 The core of your electromagnet will be something ferrous, and capable of conducting the current. A strong iron nail or door-hinge pin will do the trick.

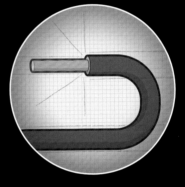

STEP 2 Find some copper wiring (it's used in many electrical cables and extension cords. The coated kind will work best).

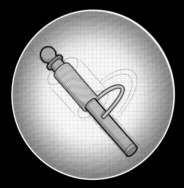

STEP 3 Wind the copper wire around the iron rod as many times as you can (more windings makes for a stronger electromagnetic field), leaving the ends free for Step 4.

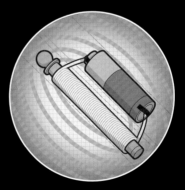

STEP 4 Attach each end of the wire to your battery terminals. The improvised electromagnet won't have much range, but anything nearby—a nearby pesky door guard's earpiece, for example—can be affected.

098 ANTI-SPY SHADES

SUNGLASSES + BATTERY + IR LED

Foiling security cameras requires staying out of the camera's sight entirely (see item 015), disguising yourself (see item 047), hacking it like Riley, or even the Jack Dalton method—although just destroying surveillance cameras will still eventually draw attention. If you have to be in the open and are camera-shy, here's how to escape detection, or at the least, facial recognition.

YOU'LL NEED

- Infrared LEDs (like those in a remote)
- Sunglasses or reading glasses
- AAA or similar size lithium batteries
- Tape
- Wire

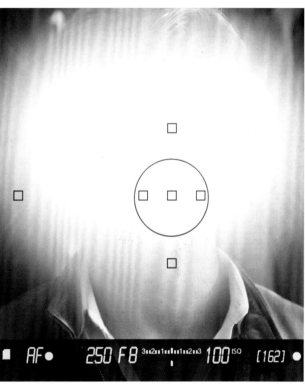

STEP 1 Tape a pair of infrared LEDs to a pair of glasses, one to each stem, just by the temple.

STEP 2 Tape a small lithium battery to the glasses just behind the LEDs.

STEP 3 Connect one terminal to the battery, leaving the other wire unconnected to save battery power until it's needed.

STEP 4 Connect the last wire between each LED and battery, and then put on your sunglasses. The intense infrared light put out by the LEDs will be invisible to the unaided eye, but since digital cameras' sensors pick up infrared (especially any night vision cameras), the light that you can't see will still easily wash out a security camera's image of your face, not to mention really annoying any unwanted paparazzi trying to snap a pic.

099 EMBASSY DEFENSE

SMOKE POWDER + OFFICE PERSONNEL

Protecting yourself in a confined location not of your choosing means working only with what's at hand. Even if you happen to find yourself at the mercy of a gang of terrorists outside an embassy, you have options. What do you have nearby to protect yourself? To fight back? To get to safety? Look for anything and everything—and then look again. An office can easily become an armory, if you just know where to look.

The stone statue by the reception desk is just waiting to be broken into bits as ammunition . . .

Raid the fax machine! Enough layers of printer paper can be effective as any armored vest (see item 115 for more).

100 BOTTLE ROCKET

BOTTLE + WATER + PRESSURE

Rocket propulsion uses reaction mass—the stuff that, in Newton's third law of motion, you throw one way in order to move in another. To be an amateur rocketeer, you'll just need a bottle, some water, and air pressure. (Fighting off Murdoc in the bargain: strictly optional.)

STEP 1 Fill your bottle about a third of the way with water and seal it with a cork. A two-liter plastic bottle is best; save the glass bottles for a last stand with a gun-toting hit man, as they can explode and spray shards everywhere if overfilled. Cardboard fins and a nose cone can improve stability, but they're not strictly necessary.

STEP 2 Insert the needle of a bicycle air pump through the cork and into the bottle, and then set the bottle upside down on the ground. Standing on the nozzle of the pump for a vertical launch (or aim it at your assailant).

STEP 3 Start pumping air into the bottle; if the seal isn't perfect, you may hear some air hissing out as it escapes. Once pressurized, when the cork is ejected (either by enough internal pressure, or manually in your standoff), the air will force out a jet of water for its reaction mass as the rocket takes flight.

101 BAKING SODA BOMB

BOTTLE + VINEGAR + BAKING SODA

The dictionary calls an explosion "a violent expansion that transmits energy outward in a shock wave." If you've been near an explosion or gunshot, you'll know exactly what they mean—an unexpected boom is a shock, indeed. Good news is, when you need to make something loud and shocking as a distraction, you don't need explosives; a few household chemicals do the job perfectly. Baking soda and vinegar foam up when mixed because the sodium bicarbonate in baking soda (a base) reacts with acetic acid in vinegar, leaving behind some water and a lot of expanding carbon dioxide gas.

YOU'LL NEED

- Empty plastic water bottle
- Vinegar
- Baking soda
- Newspaper

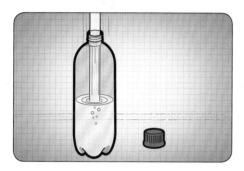

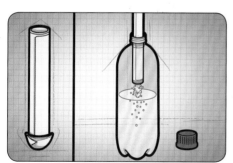

STEP 1 Open your water bottle—the thinner its walls, the better—and fill it about halfway with vinegar.

STEP 2 Pour a handful of baking soda into the bottle; or, for a more controlled method, pour some onto a sheet of newspaper, roll it up into a tube and fold its ends shut, then insert it into the mouth of the bottle.

STEP 3 Screw the cap on the bottle, and shake rapidly. As the baking soda and vinegar combine, the bottle will begin to expand; you might even feel it expanding or hear the plastic crackling.

STEP 4 Throw it fast and hard. The expanding gas combined with the jolt of impact will rupture the bottle, making some loud noise from the expanding gases, but it can still explode on its own, so you don't want to be holding this when it goes pop—or rather, bang!

102 SMOKE POWDER

COLD PACK + SALT SUBSTITUTE

Gunpowder was invented back in 300 CE in Ancient China, and it's been with us in fireworks and firearms ever since. It's a mix of three fuels: 75% saltpeter or potassium nitrate (KNO_3, also an oxygen source); 15% carbon (C), aka charcoal; and 10% sulfur (S), which helps carbon burn easier. If you need powder in a pinch (such as in a besieged embassy; see item 099), check your first-aid kits and office kitchens. The chemical inside instant cold packs creates an endothermic reaction normally, but with a little work, it becomes the source of an exothermic reaction instead: Saltpeter, the main ingredient in gunpowder.

YOU'LL NEED

- Instant cold packs
- Digital scale with metric readings (for precise weights)
- Potassium-based (KCl) salt substitute
- Clean glass jars or bottles
- Sugar
- Coffee filters
- Clean empty tin can (optional)
- Graduated beaker or cylinder (for precise volumes)

STEP 1 Cut open a cold pack and remove the interior packet containing ammonium nitrate (NH_4NO_3). Check the container label before cutting open a packet; some cold packs use urea (CH_4N_2O), which won't work for this formula at all.

STEP 2 Weigh 1.4 oz (40 g) of that ammonium nitrate, and dissolve it into 0.4 cups (100 mL) of water. Any excess crystals will not dissolve and can be filtered out, but excess water will dissolve more of the crystals.

STEP 3 Measure out 1.3 oz. (37 g) of the salt substitute into a glass jar or metal can. Pour the dissolved ammonium nitrate through a coffee filter and into the container.

STEP 4 Bring the solution to low heat, stirring continuously to dissolve the salt substitute. If your container is microwave safe, heat the solution in thirty-second intervals, stirring thoroughly between each cycle, until everything is dissolved.

STEP 5 Put the solution in a freezer for half an hour to two hours. As the solution cools, the potassium chloride (KCl) in the salt substitute will react with the ammonium nitrate, and saltpeter crystals will form and precipitate out of the solution.

STEP 6 Ammonium chloride (NH_4Cl) is dissolved in the water as a byproduct of the chemical reaction. Pour this solution out of the jar (it's used as plant fertilizer and should be safely disposed of), and then remove the saltpeter crystals to fully dry in a well-ventilated area.

STEP 7 Crush the saltpeter crystals into powder (E) and thoroughly mix them with an equal weight of sugar (F). Remember, this stuff is most of what gunpowder is, so it's flammable; exercise caution. These two ingredients can also fuel a slow-burning smoke bomb (see item 084), but if packed into a confined space such as a cannon, this crude gunpowder can still deliver a boom!

103 EXPLODING DART

"What good are bullets without a gun?" It sounds like a Zen riddle, right? But even if you're short on firearms, bullets are still worth salvaging in a crisis, whether you want a loud distraction or are cornered by a menacing hit man. (If you're interested in more things you can do with a gun or bullets on their own, see item 129.) One bullet and a ballpoint pen are nearly everything you need to make a dart that does more than just score points on a cork board.

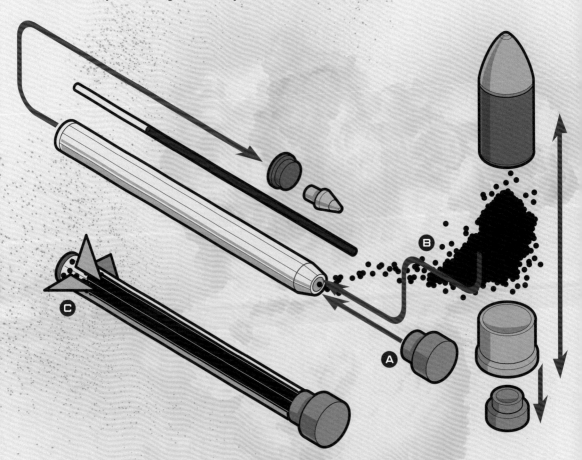

STEP 1 Empty a ballpoint pen tube of its contents.

STEP 2 Carefully remove the primer from the bullet's casing, and push it into place on the tip of the pen (A), with its striking surface facing forward.

STEP 3 Remove the slug from the bullet, and pour the gunpowder into the barrel of the pen (B).

STEP 4 Cut or fold a few pieces of paper into small triangular fins, and tape them to the barrel (C).

STEP 5 Take aim and throw. The fins will keep the dart stable, and when its head impacts a hard surface, the primer will ignite and set off the gunpowder. It won't propel a slug, but the confined interior plus pyrotechnic material definitely spells a tiny explosion!

104 STONE SLING

ROPE + ROCK

One of the most ancient weapons in existence, the sling has seen use worldwide from prehistoric times all the way up to the modern era. You can make one with nothing more than a sturdy belt holding a rock, but an even more effective sling is surprisingly easy to make. The best stones for slinging are smooth, golf ball-sized ones such as pebbles from a river, but in the right hands, a sling can be used to launch anything from marshmallows to molotovs!

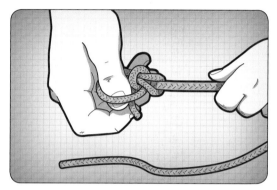

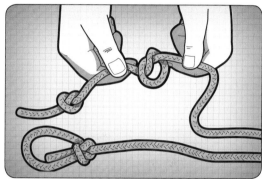

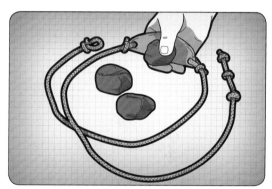

STEP 1 Measure a length of cord about the width of your arm span, and cut it in half.

STEP 2 To make the cup, cut a scrap of leather or heavy fabric, and cut a small hole in each side. Tie the cords to the scrap through its holes. (A tight bowline is ideal; see Essential Knots, Chapter 3.)

STEP 3 Tie a stopper knot in the end of one cord, and a bowline at least the size of your forefinger in the other. Be sure the two are the same distance from the cup.

STEP 4 Load a stone into the cup, slip the loop over your forefinger, and hold the stopper knot between your neighboring fingers. Depending on the size of the cup and your ammunition, it might help to have multiple stopper knots to choose from, to fine-tune a balanced grip on the stone in the cup.

STEP 5 Spin up your sling with several revolutions before launching, or use a single forward whipping motion, letting go of the stopper knot to cast your ammunition. It takes practice to time your release, but you'll zero in on your target in no time.

CHAPTER 5

REPAIRS
+RESCUES

BRINGING IT ALL TOGETHER

If you want to be like MacGyver and save the day, you kind of need to know, well, everything. But even more than knowing how everything works, you need to know how it all fits together. That's where the real power of MacGyver happens. It's combining elements of chemistry with mechanical devices and electrical devices. Building these conceptual bridges sometimes means diving into science topics that you don't think are important. But the fact is, you never know what's important until you need it.

LOOK TO THE SKIES You might think that astronomy isn't useful unless you are going into space. Not true. In fact, humans have been using the motion of objects in the sky to figure out where they are on the Earth for a long time.

Let's start with the basics—the sun and the Earth. The Earth orbits our sun once every 365 days (approximately), which is what we call a year. During this time, the Earth is also rotating on its own axis. The time it takes to rotate is 24 hours—that's a day. But wait! One very important feature of the way the Earth orbits and rotates: Its axis of rotation is tilted 21 degrees with respect to the orbital plane. Knowing that, we can use the movement of the sun and Earth system to find our location on the planet's surface.

We measure position on the Earth with two essential values: longitude and latitude. It's way easier to find latitude—you just need to measure an angle. If you imagined a giant line passing through the Earth's axis of rotation, it would point right towards the North Star (in the handle of the Little Dipper constellation). There is nothing special about this star except for its fortuitous location in the sky. If you were at the North Pole, this star would be directly overhead. At the equator, it would sit right on the horizon. So, by measuring the angle of this star above the horizon, you get your latitude.

Longitude, on the other hand, is a bit more complicated. Since the Earth is curved, the sun will be at its highest point (we call this *local noon*) in the sky at different times for different locations. If you know the actual time of local noon at one point on the Earth you can compare that to the time of noon at your point to find your longitude. This is a super difficult problem if you don't have a clock. With a clock, it's not so bad.

CREATE YOUR OWN ELECTRICITY We use electricity all the time. Nearly everyone uses things such as air conditioners, TVs, computers, dishwashers—oh, and lights. We use these things so much that we take them for granted. But what if you need to make your own electricity? How do you do that? Well, there are several options for large scale electricity plants. You've probably

heard of coal, nuclear, wind, and hydroelectric power plants. They seem very different, but really they aren't. All of these use the same principle to generate electricity: they spin an electric motor. Yes, an electric motor can be used as a generator. The only difference between these power production methods is the means by which the generator is turned.

Coal burning and nuclear power both heat water into steam and the steam turns the generator. You could also turn this generator with wind or water (as in hydroelectric). But how does a generator actually produce electricity? The answer is magnetic induction. Here's how it works: If you take a magnet and put it near a loop of wire, nothing happens. However, if you quickly remove the magnet, a brief electric current is created by the change in the field. In the case of a generator, there is a whole spinning coil of wire near a magnet; its movement continuously fluctuates the field in the magnet in order to create electricity. Induction also works to adjust current; altering the components shifts the balance of volts and amps. By creating and adjusting current, you can charge a phone or even weld metal (see item 127) on a world-saving mission.

FIRE

One of the most dangerous and destructive forces in existence, fire is made of just three things—heat, fuel, and oxidizer—but it's capable of turning everything from top secret documents to tree-filled forests to ash. It's also one of civilization's building blocks: it warms us, cooks food, refines metal, lights our way, and more. Whether you're in a survival scenario, a field op, or just an everyday situation, having at least one way to bring the heat can be useful in ways both expected and unanticipated.

LIGHTERS Practically a modern miracle, lighters pack fire making into one tiny tool: Liquid or compressed gas fuel in a sealed container that has a flick wheel or a piezoelectric trigger to create sparks. Miniaturized torch varieties make a hard jet of blue fire instead of a soft lambent flame.

PRIMITIVE SOURCES Favored by rioting mobs, a torch is just a relatively green stick or metal rod, wrapped tightly in cloth on one end to make a wick with liquid fuel soaked into it. Lamps, candles, and lanterns swap the stick for a bowl or jar, with the fuel and wick inside.

SPARKS Every fire starts with a single spark, so look for materials that can make some for you, such as a chunk of quartz and the blade in an SAK, or a flint and steel. Even the wheel on an empty lighter can crank out sparks for a good long time.

FRICTION If you can rub two sticks together, you can make fire. It takes effort, but you can lay a piece of wood flat, stand another dry stick upright on it, and spin or scrape its end on the flat wood to create embers.

ELECTRICITY
When electricity meets resistance, it turns from current to heat—and you can use this to your advantage. If you have a small battery and a length of wire (like the type in toasters), all you need then is fuel. Steel wool, rubbed with a 9-volt's contacts, is another perfect example of instant electricity-based fire.

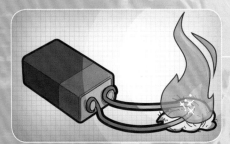

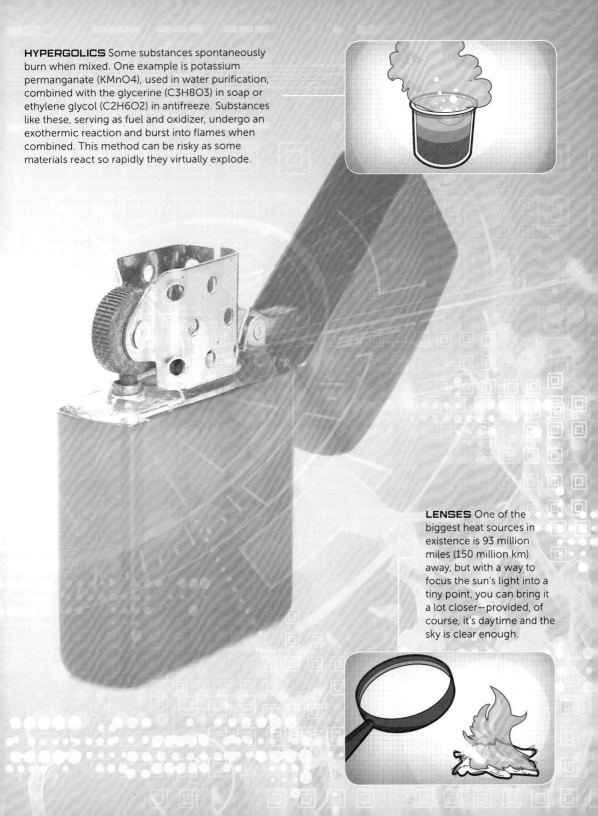

HYPERGOLICS Some substances spontaneously burn when mixed. One example is potassium permanganate ($KMnO_4$), used in water purification, combined with the glycerine ($C_3H_8O_3$) in soap or ethylene glycol ($C_2H_6O_2$) in antifreeze. Substances like these, serving as fuel and oxidizer, undergo an exothermic reaction and burst into flames when combined. This method can be risky as some materials react so rapidly they virtually explode.

LENSES One of the biggest heat sources in existence is 93 million miles (150 million km) away, but with a way to focus the sun's light into a tiny point, you can bring it a lot closer—provided, of course, it's daytime and the sky is clear enough.

105 DESSICATOR
JAR + CELL PHONE

Waterlogged electronics are dead electronics, so to have a chance at reviving them, you have to start by drying them out. Start with the most basic important: Get your phone out of the water. Take it apart if you can, or at least pull the battery, then thoroughly wipe everything dry and shake off and blow out any water you can, until you're left with residual moisture. If you're somewhere warm and dry, you're a step ahead already; if you have open air, it's best to just let things dry naturally, but in a damp or cold environment, isolate your wet electronics somewhere away from those surroundings. A plastic bag or jar is ideal, as long as it's at least a half gallon, large enough to hold the item with plenty of space to spare.

Now, for the other half: absorbing moisture. You need to soak up any remaining water, so you need material with a lot of porous surface area to speed absorption. Dried wood works well, especially splinters, shavings, or sawdust—as greater surface area means more absorption—but you'll have to get the dust out afterward. Other materials such as oatmeal or silica gel—found in kitty litter crystals or those absorbent dessicating packets with new electronics—are good, but instant rice is the best. (Regular dried rice is nowhere near as effective.) In a half-gallon container, at least four cups will be ideal, with enough space for your electronics and enough volume for air circulation in the container.

106 BRIDGED FUSE

NAIL + FUSE BOX

Fuses are made to fail and break an electrical connection in a circuit if there's a damaging power surge, but you might find yourself in a situation where replacements are hard to find. If you need to keep power going to an important system temporarily (like your old beater car's fuel pump) and you're willing to take the risk, you can actually bridge the connection with a nail or other conductive small bit of metal—even an empty foil chewing gum wrapper.

Keep in mind, this is risky for multiple reasons. Without a fuse as a safety, you may overload and burn out components, or start electrical fires; even the foil in a gum wrapper can temporarily hold enough current instead of burning away. You also risk burning or electrocuting yourself painfully, at the least. Do this only if you have no other alternative—and never with a home utility box or other structure. (See Could I Do That?!, Chapter 4, on why you really shouldn't.)

107 AIR PURIFIER

BOX FAN + FILTER

Since we all need oxygen to breathe, air quality can be a serious concern at times, whether we're dealing with pollution from wildfires, a smoggy day, or being confined aboard a ship after battling a maritime blaze. Luckily, with just a couple of common items, you can whip up your own air purifier in no time.

YOU'LL NEED

- Cardboard
- 20-inch box fan
- 20-inch HEPA filters (MERV rating 11 or higher)

STEP 1 Cut two triangular sections of cardboard to fit the top or bottom edges of the fan and filters.

STEP 2 Arrange your fan and filters upright in a triangle shape, making sure that the directional arrow on the filters points toward the fan's intake side.

STEP 3 Securely tape the edges of the filters and fan, then tape one cardboard triangle to the top of this assembly, followed by the bottom triangle. (Optionally, three filters and two squares can make a cube shape, or you can use one filter on the fan's intake side, though it's much less efficient.)

STEP 4 Plug in your fan and turn it on! A mild vacuum effect will draw smoke, dust particles, and other airborne debris to the filters, and the purified air will be blown out by the fan.

108 PERISTALTIC PUMP

DRILL + BUCKET + HOSE

A peristaltic pump works by compressing alternating segments of a flexible conduit—or, more simply, like squeezing a tube of toothpaste. The working parts never make contact with whatever passes through, so there's no contamination risk (which is why they're used in dialysis and IV machines), and this pump type can even handle viscous fluids such as concrete. Need to draw up heavy fuel from the tanks of a stranded ship to a backup generator, or maybe create a fancy drink dispenser at your next party? Grab a power drill and a few spare parts!

YOU'LL NEED

- 5-gallon (19-L) bucket
- Power drill
- Rubber hose or tubing
- Duct tape
- Luggage casters
- Wood block
- T-nut and screws

STEP 1 Cut most of a 5-gallon (19-L) bucket down, leaving about 3 inches (7.5 cm) of depth. Drill a hole in the center, and then cut two rectangular holes in either side, as wide as your hose and at least twice that in length.

STEP 2 Create the case for your pump: Slip the hose through both openings, fitting it along the inside wall of the bucket, and duct-tape the hose to the outside of the bucket at entry and exit.

STEP 3 Test-fit your casters inside the bucket—you need at least two, but four is better—by pressing the hose firmly under their wheels against the inside of the bucket, and measure the distance between casters opposite each other. Cut a piece of wood into a flat square shape to fit in the center of the bucket and hold the casters in place.

STEP 4 Assemble the rotor: Attach the casters to the edges of the block. Drill a hole in the center of the wood block to match the hole in the bucket and drive a T-nut into the hole, then screw a hex-head bolt into the T-nut.

STEP 5 Place the rotor inside the case, fitting the hose in line under the wheels, and anchor the rotor with a washer and a nut on the underside of the cassette. Put the intake end of the hose into your fluid of choice and put the output end where you want the fluid to go.

STEP 6 Attach a bolt driver head to the power drill and use it to get the rotor spinning inside the case. The fluid you're pumping should be drawn up as the rotors flatten the hose in segments and will pulse steadily along with each turn of the rotor.

ESSENTIAL KNOTS

LARK'S HEAD
Easily made and easily tied, the lark's head is a simple knot used for tying rope onto large objects, hauling heavy loads, attaching luggage tags, and even weaving friendship bracelets. It's also the basis for other knots that use a similar configuration. It's a sturdy, useful knot, but can fail if unequal force is applied to the rope's ends.

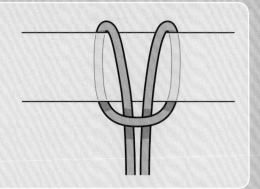

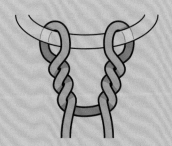

CAT'S PAW
Uses two or three (or more) twists in the bights.

USED FOR More tension and grip on the object tied by the rope.

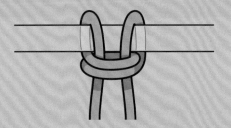

REINFORCED HITCH
Adds a half hitch in the middle.

USED FOR Improved grip with rope's friction against itself. (Can also be combined with a cat's paw or prusik.)

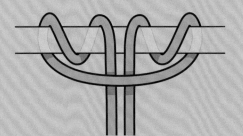

PRUSIK
Holds in place tightly under tension; can be moved when unloaded.

USED FOR Rappelling or hauling, used as a ratchet-type device.

SHEEPSHANK

To shorten rope without cutting and re-tying it, a sheepshank is ideal. Both ends have loops that other ropes or connections can be passed through, and it is best used on older or rougher ropes. A sheepshank is highly resistant to jamming, but it can come apart easily with too much or too little tension.

BELL RINGER

Uses a half hitch at only one end; immediately spills under tension.

USED FOR Keeping excess rope bundled out of the way for quick access.

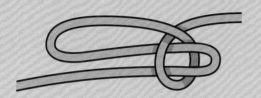

DOGSHANK

Ends of the rope run through its own loops; must have one end free to tie or untie.

USED FOR Saving rope length while avoiding spillage; weaving into a hammock or sling.

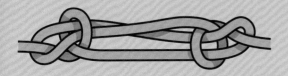

KAMIKAZE

Made like a sheepshank; the middle of rope is then cut loose while the knot is under tension.

USED FOR Saving rope after rappelling by shaking the knot once unloaded; so named because it's very unsafe and a last resort. (If you don't need rope after a descent, see item 064.)

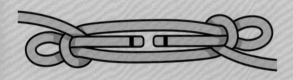

109 WATER PURIFIER
BOTTLE + WOOD + PLASTIC BAG

The average human needs a couple of liters of water per day; more if it's hot or you're exerting yourself. In the wild, finding water can be the difference between life and death from dehydration, but drinking untreated water has risks, like *shigella*, *salmonella*, *cholera*, *E. coli*, or other bacteria and parasites that can leave you weakened by illness and (thanks to water loss from diarrhea) further dehydration. If you can't make fire to boil water, and you lack other filtering methods, you can still greatly reduce the risk of infection with nothing more than a pine tree branch. A tree's internal woody tissues, called xylem, can filter out anything over 70 nanometers—including 99 percent of bacteria. Here's how to make your water safer.

STEP 1 Cut a branch from a live pine tree, and strip the bark from its surface. Saw a slice of wood from the branch, about an inch (2.5 cm) thick.

STEP 2 Fill a bottle with water from a natural source and cap its top with the slice of wood. Fit the mouth of a second, empty bottle on the other side.

STEP 3 Tightly tie a plastic bag or piece of plastic wrap around the wood piece and the bottle openings; heat-shrink it with a lighter if you can to seal everything together even more securely.

STEP 4 Invert the assembly so that the bottle of untreated water is on top, and wait. Any particles that are smaller than the filter's pores, such as salts or other minerals or contaminants, will still be present, and it'll take time for water to filter through and begin dripping into the bottom bottle. But if you leave this setup in the open while the filtering process takes place, ultraviolet radiation from sunlight can even destroy any remaining viruses (which are much smaller than bacteria and can still pass through the xylem filter). But be patient, and soon enough, you'll be rewarded with a much more potable water source.

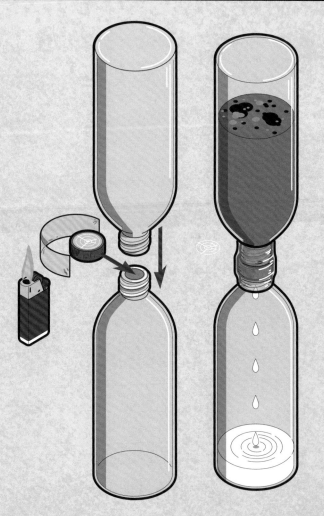

110 ROPE RESCUE LIFT
ROPE + STICK

One of the six "simple machines" defined in the Renaissance Era, a screw's mechanical advantage increases based on the ratio of its circumference versus its pitch. In other words, more threads in a given length means more power. Instead of extending like a jack screw (see item 030), this machine shortens in length. The rope's flexibility and tensile strength allow you to translate rotation into linear motion, pulling a weight as its helices tighten with each twist in the rope. You may not have to raise heavy canoes to aid fire ant–swarmed villagers in the Amazon, but the mechanical advantage in this mechanism can come in handy in plenty of other places.

STEP 1 Throw a rope over a beam, thick branch, or other sturdy fixed object overhead.

STEP 2 Tie the rope's ends together in a single loop (such as a bowline; see Essential Knots, Chapter 3) around the object.

STEP 3 Insert a sturdy wooden stick or metal bar between the ropes.

STEP 4 Begin turning the stick, and the rope will twist into a helix. Continue and the twists will tighten further, pulling and lifting the heavy object below.

STEP 4 If you're lifting a lengthy object, repeat the process at both ends; if you're lifting the mass from its center of gravity, brace it so that it lifts instead of spinning—and if there's someone trapped beneath, now's a really good time to pull them to safety.

111 CAPTIVE BOLT GUN

PIPE + SPRING + TREPHINE

Breaking through safety glass isn't easy—it's made resistant to shattering, after all. That's why firefighters use special equipment to concentrate the force of a strike on a single point, such as window-breaking tools or the back point of a fire axe. In some cases, you can even use a hard metal or ceramic object such as a spark plug. But if all you have is spare bedding parts and antique medical equipment, you can still break a window or two by creating a captive bolt gun: a device that propels a pointed metal object held in a short tube.

YOU'LL NEED

- Spring
- Pipe
- Solid steel tool with a small point (such as a screwdriver or medical trephine tip)
- Metal rod

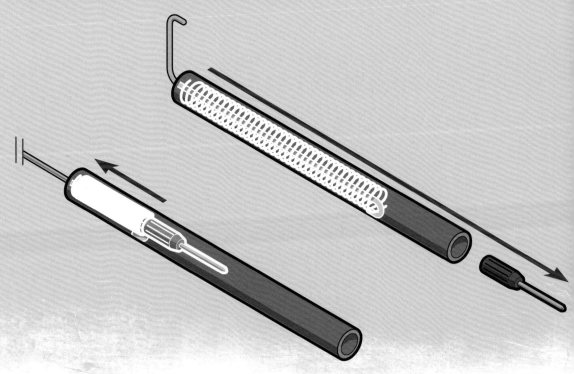

STEP 1 Test-fit a strong metal spring inside your pipe, along with a metal tool, such as a trephine (or screwdriver) to deliver the strike. Make sure that the tool's base or handle will rest against the end of the spring instead of falling inside the spring's coil.

STEP 2 Bend the end of a metal rod into a hook to grab onto the back end of the tool—or the end of the spring where it meets the tool—and thread it through the back end of the pipe. Ensure it's long enough to both reach the far end of the spring fully extended, with enough length for a handle (see next step).

STEP 3 Bend the other end of the metal rod into a handle, so that you can pull on it and compress the spring inside the pipe as you draw it back. (If the back end of the pipe is large enough that the spring can slip out, a threaded pipe and end-cap with a hole big enough to fit the rod through, will keep it contained.)

STEP 4 Slip the tool into the business end of the pipe, aim the pipe against the glass, and pull the handle to coil the spring. Once you release the handle, the tool will be shot forward with all the power of the spring behind it, focused to one point.

112 BOLT CUTTERS
SAK SCISSORS + STICK

Archimedes said, "Give me a place to stand, and a lever long enough, and I will move the world." He was right; with the mechanical advantage from the right distance and the fulcrum for a lever (another of the "simple machines"), you can move just about anything. The distance from a pivot point acts as a force multiplier, which is how bolt cutters work: That wide easy swing of the long handles translates to the tiny powerful closing of its jaws. Here's a way to turn leverage into power.

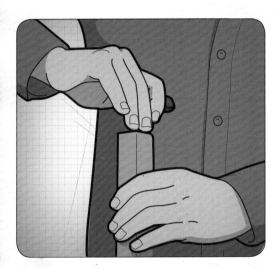

STEP 1 Use the awl tool on your Swiss Army knife to drill a hole straight into the end of a sturdy stick, just big enough to fit the scissors' handle.

STEP 2 Fold out the scissors on your Swiss Army knife, and insert the free handle into the hole you drilled into the stick. (You can also use the pliers.)

STEP 3 Hold the stick in one hand and the handle of the Swiss Army knife in the other, and use the extra leverage from the stick to apply more cutting force. You might need new scissors, depending on what you cut them with, but if you have to, say, cut through a heavy wire snare wrapped around someone's neck, it's a worthy sacrifice.

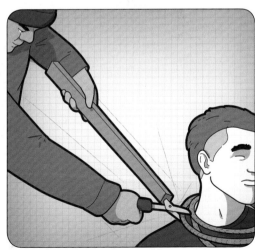

EXPLOSIONS

An explosion is defined as a near-instant release of energy, often in the form of a wave of high-temperature and high-pressure gases, and light. At subsonic speeds, low explosives create what's called a deflagration; if the shockwave moves faster than the speed of sound, it's from a high explosive, and known as a detonation.

Basic physics tells us that force involves mass times acceleration. The most important aspect of an explosion is its force, termed "brisance" (from the French word *briser*, "to break"), its capability to shatter objects from the shockwave of the blast. This translates to detonation pressure, determined by the velocity of the blast (how fast the explosion expands) and by the density (or mass) of the exploding compound, and thus, how much energy is released from it.

TNT, invented in 1863 in Germany by a scientist named Julius Wilbrand, is the standard by which all other explosives are measured. One of the most powerful explosive substances in the world is called PETN; incidentally, it's also used as a heart medication similar to nitroglycerine, the famed unstable explosive invented by Italian chemist Ascanio Sobrero in 1847 before Alfred Nobel figured out how to turn it into dynamite in 1867. (For transporting unstable explosives, see item 124).

FLOUR FIREBALL

FLOUR + ALARM CLOCK + BATTERY

You might have heard of grain explosions before. In the confines of an old tall tower, the three ingredients for fire are all available: heat from the sun beating down on the roof, oxygen in the air, and plenty of fuel from grain dust floating around. All that dust, with its huge surface-to-mass ratio, means it burns faster than most solid fuel. In that confined space, the air dense with dust, a sudden conflagration means a big change in air temperature and pressure—in other words, an explosion. The same thing happens with flour dust in some kitchen fires, only a lot smaller and less violent, and in coal mines, only a whole lot worse. The ignition source can be just a single spark or match; if you need to drive back pursuers, this is bound to do the trick.

STEP 1 Fill the confines of your escape route with flour dust. A couple of industrial-sized bags, sliced open on the run, will create both an airborne powder trail and a fuel source.

STEP 2 Find an old alarm clock, and wrap the ends of two short lengths of wire around its hands. Attach the free ends of the wires to the terminals of a battery, then wind the clock so that its hands will align with each other in a short amount of time.

STEP 3 Once the hands move into alignment, the wires will generate a spark or hot spot, and lead to a chain reaction and a room full of flames. Set the clock down close to your dust cloud before it all settles, then run! When the wake-up call you've set goes off, anyone nearby is in for a really rude awakening.

114 GSW PATCH

ID CARD + TAPE

In the event of a piercing wound to the torso, especially in the case of a gunshot sound (GSW), the victim's chest may end up filling with air if a lung is punctured. Air fills the space between ribs and lung, collapsing it and compressing the heart. This is called a tension pneumothorax, or a sucking chest wound. You can help it suck less, though: The idea behind fixing a pneumothorax is to let the air out of the injury instead of letting in more, thus a need for a one-way flow of air. Even without a one-way valve on a needle, you can still provide aid. An airtight covering is the first thing you need (let's say a borrowed ID card), followed by a way of keeping it in place (some heavy-duty tape). Cover the wound, secure the covering around its edges, with at least one edge left free. Done right, an indrawn breath should keep the seal over the wound, and an exhalation should relieve some of the pressure on the lung. After that, we recommend you get to a hospital pronto!

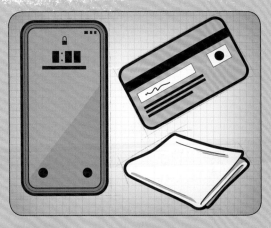

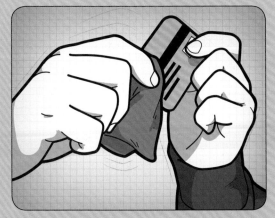

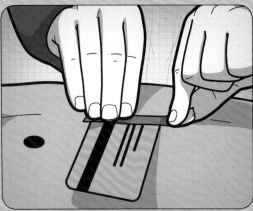

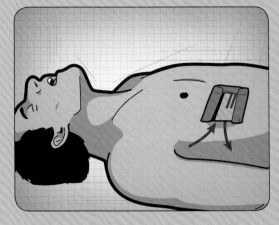

115 PHALANX

DOOR + KEVLAR

To protect themselves from arrows, slings, and other attacks, Greek and Roman soldiers would link their shields into a single wall. Modern troops and peace officers don't usually have shields, but if facing the firepower of an assault rifle (such as in item 099), you need some serious protection.

CONSIDER KEVLAR The aramid fiber layers in a kevlar vest mean serious ballistic protection; only military-grade vests can fend off AK-47 rounds for long, but they don't cover your whole body.

SHOW THEM THE DOOR Your average modern wood door is hollow-cored, with thin surface panels. Steel doors offer more protection, but only the highest rated, such as those for banks and government buildings, will resist automatic weapons fire.

LAYER UP You won't find ballistic shields unless you're in a SWAT team or other specialized force, but every layer of protection—such as kevlar and steel together—adds to your defense.

116 PAPER SHIELD

PAPER + BULLET

Kevlar is great armor, but vests only fit one to a person, and don't cover everything. But paper is a much more common material, and it can still protect you. An AK-47 bullet carries about 1,500 foot-pounds (2,300 Newton-meters) of energy, and travels at about 2,300 feet per second (700 m/s). Having done the math—and live testing—we've found it takes 2,000 to 2,500 sheets of paper to absorb that energy and stop the bullet cold. Four or five reams is all you need

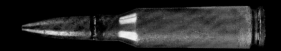

If this sounds far-fetched, keep in mind that President Theodore Roosevelt was once shot on his way to making a speech by a would-be assassin wielding a Colt .38-special police revolver in 1912. Roosevelt survived the attempt after the bullet was slowed by his speech: Fifty pages folded in half in his pocket. People might still be awaiting the advent of the "paperless office," but this is one reason to be glad we're not quite there yet.

DIY SEXTANT

CARDBOARD + TWINE

Long before modern electronic navigation existed, sailors and other travelers around the world had to figure out where they were by observing the sky and basing their location on the position of the stars. If you're somewhere a GPS signal doesn't reach, follow in the footsteps of historic explorers instead, by crafting a navigation tool to help figure out where in the world you are: a sextant.

STEP 1 Tape a short length of twine to a piece of cardboard midway along one edge.

STEP 2 Hold a pencil at the end of the twine and draw a half-circle on the cardboard with it, using the string as its radius. Cut the half-circle out of the cardboard, with the string still attached.

STEP 3 Mark 10-degree increments on the half-circle from 0° to 90° and back to 0°. (A watch dial centered on the string's attached end helps with accuracy; every 20 minutes is equal to 10 degrees.)

STEP 4 Tape a straw to the half-circle's top edge as a sight, and hang a paperclip from the twine.

118 CELESTIAL NAVIGATION

SEXTANT + WATCH + RADIO

Finding one's exact location on the globe was a major challenge for early explorers until the invention of the sextant and modern chronometer, along with the discovery of calculus. Even with the advent of GPS, navigation by observing the stars and sun is still important: It works worldwide without power, creates no electronic signals for an enemy to track, and (unless it's cloudy) it can't be jammed by an enemy either. The most accurate navigation requires some serious calculus and an almanac with daily celestial notes, but if you're stranded on a desert island, or maybe just the desert far outside Area 51, you can still get a good idea of your location.

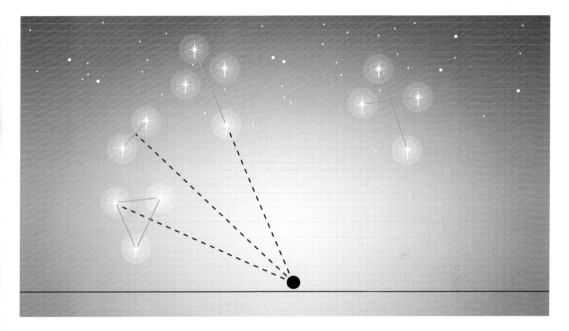

STEP 1 Aim a sextant at the star Polaris in the Northern Hemisphere. If you're in the Southern Hemisphere, look for Sigma Octantis (found by tracing the intersection of two lines from the Southern Cross and the midpoint of the Southern Triangle). Record the observed angle on the sextant.

STEP 2 Subtract the angle found in Step 1 from 90 to find your approximate latitude.

STEP 3 Drive a stick upright into a level surface. Measure the length of the shadow cast by the stick close to noon, and every 1 to 5 minutes before and after, and note the recorded time for each. The time matching the shortest measurement will give you your local noontime.

STEP 4 If you know what time zone you're in, compare the difference from Greenwich Meridian Time; add (or subtract, if you're east of GMT) the minutes before or after 12:00 recorded in Step 3 to find approximate longitude. For example, in the Eastern time zone (five hours behind GMT), with a shortest measurement at 12:04, gives you five hours and four minutes. Each hour equals 15 degrees' rotation, so your longitude would be roughly 76 degrees west of the meridian.

STEP 5 If you don't know your time zone, tune a radio to 2.5, 5, 10, or 20 MHz: These worldwide high-frequency channels broadcast regular GMT announcements. Compare your local time; use the same measurements as in Step 4 to find longitude.

COULD I DO THAT?!

Vehicle airbag safety systems are built from a few combined elements: accelerometers that measure changes in velocity from sudden impacts, a set of explosive charges, and the wiring between the two. When your car rapidly decelerates on impact or is hit hard enough, the accelerometer sends a signal to a detonator, which ignites an explosive charge that fills the airbag with inert gas in a fraction of a second.

The airbag itself isn't likely to damage anything, but can cause some minor injuries, and the force of a car's dashboard panel blown off by the inflating airbag has been known to shatter windshields. There are also very rare cases of malfunctioning or damaged inflators basically becoming small pipe bombs as the blast fragments the metal casing.

Trapped in a buried SUV with Riley and Dalton, Mac extracted an inflator without its airbag from inside the door panel, and braced it by the windshield so the blast channeled through the inflator would directly impact the glass. He also told Riley and Dalton to take cover and guard their ears—a smart move in a confined area, because an explosion means flying debris, and the blast pressure can rupture eardrums (See item 079.)

Could you do this yourself? Possibly, but with a lot of risk. Any confined space increases the power of an explosion, and thus the risk of injury or fatality. You'd have to know how to remove and set off the inflator, where and how to position it for maximum effect, and protect yourself from the explosion—all technical skills and safety lessons MacGyver acquired from his days in EOD.

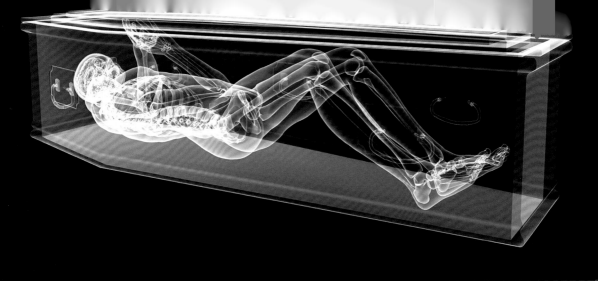

119 LIVE BURIAL ESCAPE

COFFIN + RESOLVE

The technical term for a premature burial is known as "vivisepulture," a form of punishment or torture used throughout history. Being buried alive is a common and understandable phobia: You're in a dark, cramped space with a limited air supply, and a lot of heavy earth overhead. That said, if you're interred in a coffin (or entombed in an automobile) by a sadistic villain and still breathing, it won't be easy, but might you still have at least a chance to rescue yourself, even if you weren't buried with explosive charges.

SAVE YOUR BREATH Depending on how much space you take up inside a coffin, you'll have at least an hour's worth of air during your escape attempt. A vehicle means a deeper grave, but with more air, workspace, and time. Eventually, though, carbon dioxide buildup will lead to drowsiness, unconsciousness, and suffocation, so you're on the clock. Breathe slowly to keep calm and save oxygen.

FIND A WEAK POINT Focus on one spot in the midline of the coffin lid, and kick, punch, pry, or if you have your Swiss army knife, gouge at it. The lid may already be cracking from the weight of

earth overhead; if so, concentrate there to speed things up. A car's metal rooftop can withstand tons of force in a rollover, so a window is your exit strategy, especially if it's already damaged. Again, hit a central spot, using a seatbelt buckle or other metal object (see item 111) if you can.

MASK UP AND PREPARE It's already dark in here, so tie your shirt over your head as a hood to avoid mouthfuls of soil, because once the lid breaks in or the window shatters, it'll start spilling in. Pull as much broken wood or windshield glass out of the way as you need to fit through (use your socks as hand protection if you don't have gloves). Start packing dirt into the far end of the coffin or car tightly and, well . . .

DIG YOUR WAY OUT Freshly turned soil weighs about 75 pounds (34 kg) per cubic foot, and you have several feet of it above you; dig as narrowly as you can to reduce the risk of a collapse. Keep packing earth below and around you as you tunnel upward. When your fingertips breach the surface, make like a zombie—by now, you'll probably resemble one!—and claw your way free!

120 PET SPLINT

Sometimes, the most important rescues aren't crazy lifesavers. Some don't even involve humans. But the dogs, cats, and other animals that are our house pets and friends still matter, and taking care of them if they're hurt is just as important caring for any two-footed family member. If your furry friend has an injured limb and you're far from a vet, here's how to help.

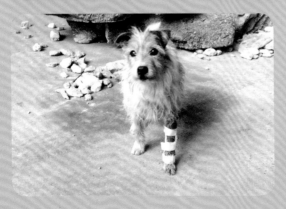

STEP 1 Move slowly and steadily so as not to startle your injured animal buddy while tending to them. Don a pair of latex or nitrile gloves, and have a look at your pet's limb to make sure there is no serious bleeding. If there is, get to a vet soon as you can, after wrapping the wound to help control the bleed. If the break is very seriously misaligned, that's another reason to get to medical help first. Otherwise, clean any injuries if possible, using clean water or saline solution, and dab gently with gauze or a clean cloth.

STEP 2 Wrap your pet's leg with gauze or bandaging material, then apply splints to either side of the limb to stabilize it; wooden tongue depressors are the perfect size for a small dog or cat, and you can cut them down easily to fit smaller limbs such as a bird's leg. Just like when treating a human patient, be sure that the splint is long enough to reach from just before one limb joint to past the next; if you're stabilizing a break high up on the leg, wrap and splint the entire limb together all the way to the shoulder or hip.

STEP 3 Add tape around the splint and gauze to hold everything together, at the top and bottom at the least, but not so tightly that the splint presses against the injury. Once you can get your pet to a veterinarian, they can be given a proper checkup, although (just like a human in a cast) they might still have to wear a splint for a few days to several weeks.

121 CRUTCHES

In an emergency (and especially in an emergency landing—see item 078) there are bound to be injured folks. If someone has a leg injury but can still move around after their limb is splinted, the next step is helping improve their mobility by taking weight off the injured leg. Here's how to create a crutch of your own.

TEND THE INJURY FIRST If your buddy has an injured foot, bandage and splint it to the ankle. If their lower leg is hurt, splint it up to the knee; a thigh, from hip to knee. Always immobilize the injury at the next joint up on the body.

GRAB A SKID (OR A STICK) You need an object that will support the weight of the person walking with the crutch, but not so heavy that they can't easily move with it. A helicopter landing skid made of a hollow aluminum tube is great—not so great for the crashed chopper maybe—but a sturdy branch with a wide forked end is also ideal. Cut its length to fit just below the height of the user's armpit.

ADD PADDING Walking with a crutch will be taxing, but you can make it easier with a good amount of padding for the user to rest their arm; the longer you make the pad, the more comfortable the crutch will be. Foam padding from a seat is great (and manufactured crutches use foam or foam rubber), but a bundle of cloth wrapped around the fork end or even a shirt stuffed full of moss, leaves, grasses, and other soft natural debris can work.

122 BLEEDING CONTROL

"All bleeding stops eventually" is a phrase well known in medicine, with a fairly double-edged meaning: Either it stops on its own or you have to find a way to halt blood loss before . . . well, before the injured person runs out of blood.

MILD SCRAPES Small oozing wounds often clot on their own. Even without bandages, direct pressure on the area helps, and any little wounds that keep bleeding can be stopped with a dose of pepper poured onto the wound. Both cayenne and black pepper powder help clotting, and despite their spicy taste, they have natural anti-inflammatory and pain relief properties.

MORE SEVERE CUTS Without sutures or bandages, a bigger wound can be sealed by super glue, since its active compound, cyanoacrylate, was originally for medical use. If you can, carefully rinse the injury and pat it dry, then dab super glue a little at a time until the area is covered; hold the edges of a cut together if needed while sealing it. Vein injuries, such as a serious laceration on your forearm, steadily bleed dark red blood. Elevate the wound and hold a cloth or bandage (or, if nothing else, your own hand) in place firmly for several minutes; add more bandages if they soak through.

REALLY BIG TIME BLEEDS An artery pulses bright red blood with each heartbeat. Find a pressure point (in their elbow, armpit, thigh, or groin) upward from the injury and press firmly until bleeding stops, or use a tourniquet. Rubber surgical tubing, a thick band of gauze roll, or even a belt will do. Wrap the affected limb tightly a few inches above the bleed, then tie a short, sturdy stick into the bindings, twist it even tighter, and tie it off. This will hurt a lot, and they may lose the limb without medical intervention—but there's a good reason "life before limb" is another well-known phrase in emergency medicine.

SONIC FIRE EXTINGUISHER

SPEAKER + BUCKET

A sonic fire extinguisher works by disrupting the flow of oxygen to the flames with pulses of sound, instead of cooling, wetting, or smothering the fire as with liquid or powder fire extinguishers. In December 2011, DARPA demonstrated a technique to using soundwaves for fire suppression. In 2015, a pair of college students at George Mason University in Virginia refined the design into a portable setup made with off-the-shelf components. You don't have to be near a burning wellhead for oil fields in central Africa if you want to try your hand at putting out spot fires with this device, but no matter the location, here's how to drop the bass. This kind of device can put out small fires from a few feet away—similar in scale to a mini chemical extinguisher.

YOU'LL NEED

- 2-gallon (7.6-L) plastic bucket with snap lid
- 8-inch (20-cm) round subwoofer
- Glue or tape
- Speaker wire with audio jack, or RCA-type subwoofer cable (if your portable stereo has RCA ports)
- Portable stereo

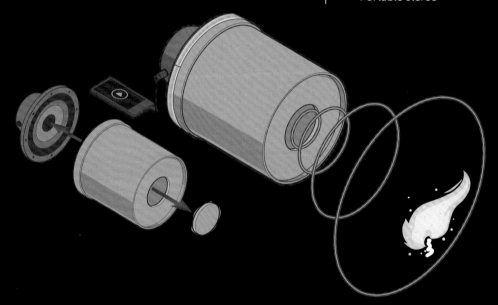

STEP 1 Measure and cut a hole in the bucket's lid to fit the diaphragm of the subwoofer and tape or glue the subwoofer securely into place.

STEP 2 Cut a circular hole in the middle of the bottom of the the bucket, roughly half the width of the bucket itself.

STEP 3 Snap the lid with its attached subwoofer into place on the bucket, and then connect the terminals on the speaker wire to the terminals of your subwoofer.

STEP 4 Plug the extinguisher assembly into your portable stereo, and turn up the volume.

STEP 4 Use a tone-generating app connected to your stereo (or pre-record tones on a disc or audio file) for a firefighting soundwave. Pulses between 30 and 60 Hertz (the number of vibrations per second), in a sawtooth-wave setting are best. The bucket acts as a collimator: The hole cut into it focuses the pulses from the subwoofer just like one of those air-blasting toys, only a lot faster. Take aim at the base of the flames, and watch the bass put them out!

124 DYNAMITE TRANSPORT

EXPLOSIVES + TRUCK + SPRINGS

Some say it's kinda ironic that the Nobel prizes came from a man who was basically an arms merchant in his era, not to mention the inventor of dynamite. But Nobel founded those prizes because he foresaw the need to advance the cause of peace—and similarly, he also created dynamite as a safer way of using nitroglycerin, the famously unstable explosive. The Nobel prizes are still going strong, but old dynamite doesn't stand the test of time so well. As it ages, dynamite takes on a waxy, greasy look as nitro 'sweats' out of the absorbent material, and this stuff really can be just as unstable as the movies portray. So how do you get a load of crates full of leaky dynamite safely to where they're needed, with miles of bad road (or no road!) ahead, in an old beater with a lack of suspension, and no sign of Roy Scheider anywhere? Here's what to consider.

START WITH STABILITY Find a wide, level surface to rest your delicate explosives on, like a sizeable wooden panel or table top that'll fit your vehicle. You don't want the crates bumping each other or sliding around, so tie them down tight.

SPRING INTO ACTION Your carrying surface needs to keep things shock-free for its unstable passengers. A set of heavy-duty industrial springs can help; they may not fit your chassis, but once attached to the wood panel like (you guessed it) legs on a table, they'll smooth out a bouncy ride.

SOAK UP SPILLS Those leaky crates are bound to end up dripping some of their contents into the open. A layer of sand or soil in the bed of your truck, under the springs and platform, act as a sponge for stray nitroglycerin. Drive cautiously!

125 RADIATOR PATCH

EGG + TRUCK

A bit of basic automotive knowledge: Your vehicle's radiator circulates fluid, shedding heat from its vanes; if your radiator fails, so does your engine as it overheats and seizes. But what if your ride to safety has a leaky radiator, you're short on tools, and you're far from an auto parts store? All you might need to do is raid a nearby chicken coop—or fridge, if there's no henhouse nearby.

Grab an egg and crack it open, then empty the egg white into the radiator's opening. The fluid inside will carry it through, and as the egg white proteins solidify from the heat, they will eventually find their way to the source of the leak, acting as a patch from the inside. It's a little bizarre, but that doesn't mean it can't work—at least temporarily, although it won't work on huge cracks or holes. And you certainly don't want to go cracking eggs into your best radiator unless necessary, so this is best used as a last-ditch attempt to keep your vehicle from overheating. But then again, you should be used to last minute saves with unconventional methods by now, right?

126 EMERGENCY GENERATOR

MOPED + ALTERNATOR

So many modern systems run on electrical power that it's almost impossible to use them in a blackout—losing all the advantages of climate-controlled, brightly-lit, sterile operating rooms in a hurricane or other natural disaster. But if you have access to at least one working motor, and a way to collect power from it, you can make your own generator and keep the lights going.

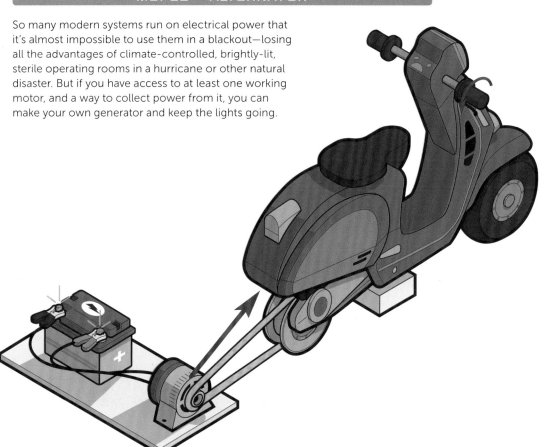

STEP 1 Park a moped close as possible to where you're going to set up your generator. Route the exhaust safely away from the area using ducting, like the kind used for dryers or furnaces.

STEP 2 Get your moped's back wheel off the ground using the kickstand (or brace it on a crate or stand), and remove the rear tire.

STEP 3 Set up at least one alternator with its axis in line with the rear wheel. Anchor it in place on a heavy wooden block or other mounting.

STEP 4 Attach a drive belt between the rear wheel and alternator; you can use heavy rubber medical

tubing or a bicycle inner tube to stretch between the two. (If you use multiple alternators, you can still turn them using one single belt, crossed over itself between alternators.)

STEP 5 Hook up the terminals of your alternator to a battery if you need to store power. Attach a DC-to-AC inverter's clamps to the battery in order to plug in any devices that need electrical power.

STEP 6 Start your moped's engine, and slowly rev the throttle to begin powering up. You can run this generator as long as you have fuel; alternatively, you can even set a bicycle in place and pedal the power out instead!

127 STICK WELDER

MICROWAVE + EXTENSION CORDS

Arc welding passes electricity through a resistant material, which heats and melt the substance by amperage, an amount of electricity conducted in a given time period. "Household" current is normally high-voltage and (somewhat) low-amperage, but a transformer changes that. Current goes in one end, to pair of wire coils. A gap between the coils, filled by a magnet, induces an electromagnetic eddy current; the difference between the number of windings in each coil changes the balance between volts and amps.

Take your average 1,000-watt (100v/10aH) microwave oven: If its transformer has two sets of 100 coils, replacing the second set with 20 would create a difference based on the 100:20 ratio, reducing voltage by 5 (to 20v), and raising amperage by 5 (to 50aH). With arc-welding tools, you can fix a broken spark plug terminal or weld metal plates onto an armored vehicle, but skill and protective equipment is necessary to avoid burns, blindness, or lethal electric shock (see Could I Do That?!, Chapter 4; and item 128). If you want to put that kind of power put to use for repairs, here's how to do it . . . very carefully.

YOU'LL NEED

- Microwave oven transformer
- 10-gauge electrical cable
- Electrical tape and wire nuts
- Jumper cables
- Welding rods
- Welding safety equipment

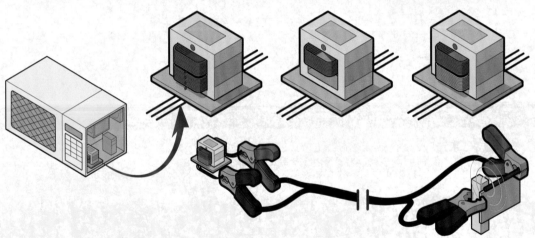

STEP 1 Open an unplugged microwave's casing and discharge its capacitor by touching its terminals with the tip of an insulated screwdriver to avoid a dangerous electric shock. Remove the power cable and transformer from the microwave.

STEP 2 Connect the microwave power cable's positive and negative leads to the terminals on the transformer's primary coils.

STEP 3 Cut the secondary coils from the core of the transformer, taking care not to damage the primary. Wind a length of 10-gauge cable around the core twenty times as a replacement coil.

STEP 4 Cut the clamps from a set of jumper cables and connect their wiring to the ends of the new secondary coils.

STEP 5 Clamp your welding parts firmly to a non-conductive surface with one cable clamp, and fit a welding rod into the jaws of the other clamp.

STEP 6 Put on safety equipment and plug in your transformer.

STEP 7 Strike an arc on the metal with the rod as if lighting a match, hold the rod's tip close to the metal, and begin your weld.

128 PROTECTIVE LENSES

DISKETTE + SAFETY GLASSES

Welding creates a lot of infrared and ultraviolet energy along with visible light, and brief eye exposure is as dangerous as staring at the sun during a solar eclipse. Light-based injury to the eye is a lot like sunburn: You may not feel it until it's too late, and it can take hours to develop. Real welding protection or eclipse-viewing tools are optimal protection, but you just might be able to shield your eyes in an emergency with an old box of floppy disks. Here's how.

READY YOUR MATERIALS Floppies store data in a thin metallic coating on a plastic sheet; this coating is what filters the light. Carefully open the casing of a floppy and remove the disk without scratching it. Hold it up to a bright light and you'll see how the coating on the plastic sheeting blocks most of the illumination.

DO A SAFETY TEST Digital cameras can see from shallow ultraviolet (350nm) to the end of infrared (1,000nm). Hold the disk between a cellphone or camera's lens and a UV light or infrared LED, such as the one at the end of a remote control. If the material doesn't dim the light's output, see item 009 or 034 instead.

PREPARE YOUR PROTECTION Trace the shape of a pair of safety glasses' lenses, and use the templates to cut the diskette material to match. Tape them in place behind the plastic lenses to protect them from debris and sparks, and discard any scratched filters.

LAYER UP Light filtering multiplies for each layer added; for example, if the light from a single filter is 10% as bright, two will cut it to 1%, and so on. Stack layers to the point of total opacity, then add more. Remove one layer at a time until you can just barely see the brightest light (such as a welding arc, which can emit five times more UV light than the sun) through them. If you're unsure of your protection, don't risk it—after all, you only have two eyes—and be as safe as possible regardless. Use every protection you can, and work in short bursts on small projects.

129 PLOWSHARES FROM SWORDS

GUN + BULLET + INGENUITY

Around 500 BCE, Laozi, the Chinese philosopher and creator of the *Tao Te Ching*, wrote, "Weapons, no matter how beautiful, are instruments of ill omen." A few centuries prior to that, the biblical Isaiah's writing urged people to "beat their swords into plowshares." This isn't to say that firearms have no real use—only that they have one intended purpose, and while the Phoenix Foundation does deploy combat-trained strike

teams (including a very well-armed Jack Dalton), you can still do a lot more with the parts and ammunition in a firearm than just shooting.

BARREL A length of high-grade steel can be a lifesaver. Safely unloaded and with the stock still attached, you have a potential walking stick for an injured buddy. On its own, a barrel can become a pry bar or a splint for an injured limb.

ACTION All the small moving parts of a gun's action can find use elsewhere. For example, pins might be useful lockpicks or other small tools; the springs can be employed in countless ways, such as replacing the broken spring in an engine's throttle linkage or cushioning a shockproof container (see item 124 for an example).

FURNITURE Built specifically as grips for holding a firearm, a stock and forend can be put to use as handles for other tools. If they're plastic or metal, they can be adapted as splints or bracings; pieces cut from wooden furniture, meanwhile, can become kindling. A hollow metal handguard around a free-floating barrel can find new life as a container, or even as the handle and fuel holder for a simple torch (see Don't Get Caught Without Fire, in this chapter).

FRAME It's mostly a solid chunk of metal, but don't let that fool you: The solid frame of a handgun or the lower receiver of a long gun can be used to brace or shim objects, be repurposed for a handle (and its handgrip is just right), or maybe even as a wrench to open a stuck coolant valve in an overheating nuclear reactor.

MAGAZINE A hollow metal container with a compressing spring inside may not sound like huge deal, but the machined metal case is, again, a container. Cut apart, its metal panels can have their edges sharpened and used as handheld blades or in a hatchet or other chopping tool, while the flexible metal spring inside is almost as versatile as any other.

AMMUNITION A treasure trove of useful parts, the bullet in a cartridge is a solid mass of metal which you can use as a small weight; if it's lead, it can be quickly reshaped into something else, even easily melted to patch a tiny gap. The propellant makes for a ready powder-trail fuse or fire-starting accelerant. The primer can become the spark for a fire or noisemaker, or set off another device (see item 103). Even the casing could be put to work as a tiny waterproof container; employed as a pick for certain locks it can fit into (see item 006); or, if flattened and given an edge, made into a small knife (see item 021 for more).

ACCESSORIES Extra handgrips equal more handles, the flashlight on a tactical rail is just as useful on its own, and a sighting laser is full of potential (see items 040, 041, and 073). If you've run out of other means, the convex lens in the scope can even focus sunlight to start a fire.

130 PLAN B

IMPROVISE!

Murphy's Law states, "Whatever can go wrong will go wrong," and let's be honest: There's a lot out there, both anticipated and unexpected, that can and will go wrong, whether in daily life, a mild emergency, or an extremely unusual and unstable situation. Eventually, even if you're crazy prepared and you have exactly the right plan and the right tool to handle the situation you're facing, there will eventually come a moment when you find your strategy won't quite apply. You'll lose a crucial part or tool, or it'll break or go missing. Something may be overlooked or forgotten. There are any number of reasons an idea will fall apart—and it's certainly daunting when changing situations make your plans infeasible.

But don't despair. Just follow Plan B: Improvise!

This manual is more than a tool to guide you through the materials and processes for scores of ideas. It'll also hopefully sharpen your thinking, and put you on a path to seeing everything in the world around you a little differently. The famous Swiss Army knife may be MacGyver's personal favorite, and it's a very useful tool indeed. But the one tool truly more adaptable, versatile, and capable than any other is your mind. (Just don't forget the paperclips!)

INDEX
+CREDITS

INDEX OF MATERIALS

FROM THE WRITER: This book wouldn't have come together without a lot of help. I'd like to thank *MacGyver* technical consultant and super fan, Doctor Rhett Allain, Ph.D, for all his invaluable knowledge and assistance that informs so much of this manual. Likewise, my thanks to everyone at Insight Editions, Weldon Owen, and elsewhere, especially Mariah Bear, Allister Fein, Conor Buckley, Laurie Ulster, Scott Erwert, Madeleine Calvi, and Juan Calle, and to Iain Morris of Cameron & Co. for early design work. And of course, my sincere gratitude to Peter Lenkov, Lucas Till, Maryann Martin, Risa Kessler, Benjamin Mitnick, Christopher Hood, and the rest of the *MacGyver* crew, and other folks at CBS.

CREDITS

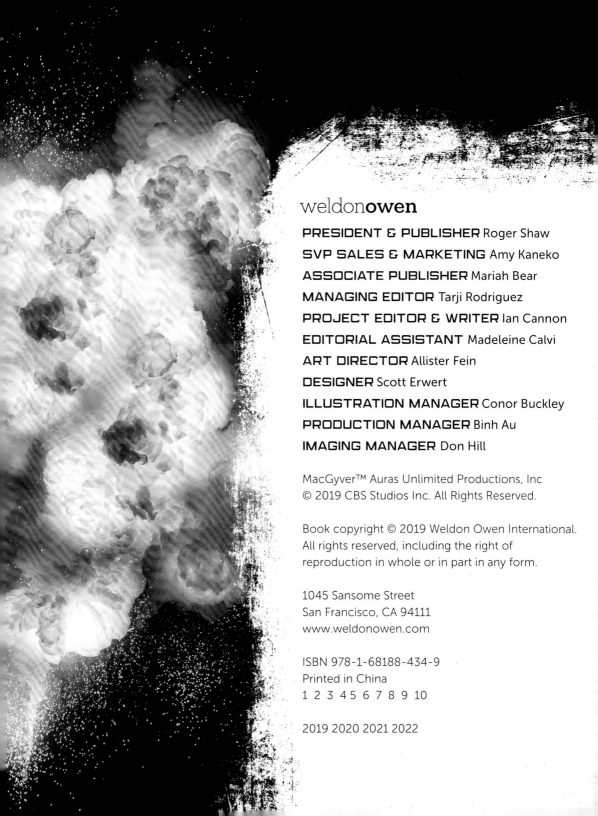

weldon**owen**

PRESIDENT & PUBLISHER Roger Shaw
SVP SALES & MARKETING Amy Kaneko
ASSOCIATE PUBLISHER Mariah Bear
MANAGING EDITOR Tarji Rodriguez
PROJECT EDITOR & WRITER Ian Cannon
EDITORIAL ASSISTANT Madeleine Calvi
ART DIRECTOR Allister Fein
DESIGNER Scott Erwert
ILLUSTRATION MANAGER Conor Buckley
PRODUCTION MANAGER Binh Au
IMAGING MANAGER Don Hill

1045 Sansome Street
San Francisco, CA 94111
www.weldonowen.com

ISBN 978-1-68188-434-9
Printed in China
1 2 3 4 5 6 7 8 9 10

2019 2020 2021 2022